Nuclear Fuel and Energy Policy

Written under the auspices of the
Center of International Studies, Princeton University

A list of other Center publications
appears at the back of this book

Nuclear Fuel and Energy Policy

S. Basheer Ahmed
Center of International Studies
Princeton University

Lexington Books
D.C. Heath and Company
Lexington, Massachusetts
Toronto

Library of Congress Cataloging in Publication Data

Ahmed, S. Basheer.
  Nuclear fuel and energy policy.

  Bibliography: p.
  Includes index.
  1. Atomic energy industries—United States.
2. Uranium industry—United States—Mathematical models.
3. Nuclear fuels—Estimates and costs. I. Title.
HD9698.U52A59   333.7   78–19673
ISBN 0–669–02714–6

Published simultaneously in Canada

Printed in the United States of America

International Standard Book Number: 0–669–02714–6

Library of Congress Catalog Card Number: 78–19673

For Ivy

Contents

List of Figures

List of Tables

Acknowledgments

The very nature of the subject and the issues in nuclear fuel require that people of various backgrounds provide suggestions, constructive reviews, and evaluation of the different sections. In the initial phase of this study I benefited a great deal from the discussions and reviews of Andrew P. Sage (engineering) of the University of Virginia and R. Koshal (economics) of Ohio University.

Several persons at Princeton University reviewed different parts of the manuscript and provided valuable suggestions. I am grateful to Frank Von Hipple (Center for Environmental Studies) for stimulating discussions and reviews on uranium resources in the United States and abroad. I also benefited from discussions with Kenneth Deffyes (geology) on uranium resources. Jan Beyea (Center for Environmental Studies) reviewed several chapters thoroughly and made numerous improvements in the text. Dan Feenberg (economics) reviewed the econometric model and made many useful suggestions in the forecasting of uranium prices. Geoffrey Watson (statistics) reviewed the algebraic formulation of resource estimation methodology. Gerald Garvey (politics) reviewed the whole manuscript for its overall contribution toward the development of nuclear energy policy. Robert Brenner (Woodrow Wilson School) has helped throughout the preparation of the manuscript and has offered many suggestions on the policy aspects of nuclear analysis. Robert Rycroft (Center of International Studies) made a thorough review of policy implications of nuclear fuel analysis, and the discussions with Rycroft helped me to evolve my own preferences for long-term nuclear options.

Several people at other institutions have contributed their efforts to the preparation of this manuscript. My sincere thanks to John C. Houghton (MIT Energy Laboratory) for reviewing thoroughly the material on the uranium mining and milling industry. Joan Greenwood (Charles River Associates) made several suggestions that improved the analysis of uranium prices. Kan Young (ECON) reviewed the econometric model of the uranium-mining industry.

None of these individuals shares responsibility for the analysis of the results and the development of the long-term nuclear strategies for the U.S. economy. I take full responsibility for the views and the results expressed in this work.

I am deeply indebted to Cyril Black for providing me with all the help and facilities at the Center for the completion of the work. It is with grateful appreciation that I wish to thank Doris Lohner for her excellent typing of all the drafts of the manuscript. Finally, this work would never have been completed without the help and understanding of my wife, Alice, who shared all the hardships through the countless hours and days.

Introduction

During the last five years there have been some dramatic changes in the energy economy of the United States. Fear of energy shortages and the growing reliance on foreign imports of oil led to a search for alternative sources of energy. Nuclear power which once promised to be the major hope as a stepping-stone for an infinite energy resource base suffered a setback in the early 1970s when environmental legislation and public resistance dampened its growth. Despite such resistance, nuclear power continues to make significant contributions to the growth of the energy economy. Although some environmental and social aspects of nuclear power have constrained its growth, some basic issues are vital to the survival of nuclear programs. The future of nuclear power rests on some of these basic issues which are still unresolved in determining the future courses of action. A major issue is the availability of uranium resource and its adequacy in meeting the future needs of nuclear capacity. Another issue is the cost of the fuel supply which may either curtail nuclear growth or diminish its economic superiority. A better understanding of uranium supplies and the cost of nuclear fuel, in the short run, will certainly help solve the dilemma of several electric utilities whether or not to build the nuclear plants. The results of the analysis should also provide some assistance in the evaluation of long-term energy alternatives.

The purpose of this book is multifold. One of the purposes is to examine thoroughly the uranium resource situation in relation to the future needs of the nuclear economy. Currently the United States is the world's leading producer and consumer of nuclear fuels. In the future U.S. nuclear choices will be highly interdependent with the rest of the world as other countries begin to develop their own nuclear programs. Therefore the world's uranium resource availability has also been examined in relation to the expected growth in the world nuclear industry.

Based on resource evaluation, the study develops an economic framework for analyzing and describing the behavior of the U.S. uranium mining and milling industry. An econometric model designed to reflect the underlying structure of the physical processes of the uranium mining and milling industry has been developed. The model establishes the relationship between the significant individual variables as well as the interactions of these relationships among the different components of the industry. The purpose of this model is to forecast uranium prices and outputs for the period 1977-2000. Because uncertainty has sometimes surrounded the economic future of the uranium markets, the results of the econometric modeling should be interpreted with great care and restrictive assumptions. This model is not the final answer to the modeling of inudstry behavior; other quantitative formulations for forecasting uranium production and prices are possible. Another aspect of this study is to provide much needed information on the operations of government-owned enrichment plants and the practices used by the government in the determination of fuel enrichment costs. This study discusses possible future developments in enrichment supply and technologies and their implications for future enrichment costs. A review of the operations involving the uranium concentrate conversion to uranium hexafluoride and fuel fabrication is also provided. An economic analysis of these costs provides a comprehensive view of the front-end costs of the nuclear fuel cycle.

The reader who is generally uninterested in the mathematical formulations may wish to skip chapters 7, 12, and 13 and read only the material on the description of the industry to form his own opinion of the policy implications concerning the future of nuclear power.

The results of the uranium price forecasts along with the expected trends in future enrichment costs, costs of conversion to UF_6, and fuel fabrication costs form the basis for some conclusions concerning the economics of the nuclear fuel cycle for the next twenty-five years. This work should be treated as an initial scientific effort in the evaluation of some complex issues that are inherent in the nuclear fuel cycle and vital to the operations and planning of the nuclear industry.

1

An Overview of the Nuclear Industry

Status of the Nuclear Industry

The emergence of the nuclear industry in the early sixties promised a bright future for the U.S. energy industry, assuring unlimited supplies of low-cost energy in the growth of the U.S. economy. Much of the optimism concerning the nuclear potential was based on the assumption of an early and smooth transition of the lightwater reactor industry into the broader phase of the plutonium economy. Recent unresolved issues relating to the economic and environmental aspects of nuclear breeders and the fear of proliferation of nuclear weapons have changed the course of the nuclear breeder economy. In particular, the recent legislation has had an impact on the entry of breeders on a commercial scale, resulting in the indefinite postponement of this energy source.

The contributions of the lightwater reactor industry in meeting the future energy needs of the U.S. economy depend on several questions pertaining to the economics of the nuclear fuel cycle. A decision to build a nuclear plant is generally made on economic criteria that must, in all cases, meet the requirements of the National Environmental Policy Act of 1969. In addition, the nuclear choice is critically dependent on the assurance of adequate supplies of uranium to fuel the lifetime needs of the reactors. Once the reactor is built, the nuclear fuel for thirty years of its operations must be guaranteed. Currently there is some uncertainty concerning the size and availability of uranium resources. The knowledge of uranium resource availability and the economic costs of supplying the required amounts of uranium will have a decisive influence on the choice between building a nuclear plant and building a coal plant. These factors have further bearing on some of the important issues regarding the emphasis placed on the research and development of the breeder programs in the United States. Several recent studies have examined various aspects of the nuclear fuel cycle industry. Some of the studies led to the support or the rejection of the thesis that the early start of the breeder is vital to the welfare of the U.S. energy economy. Currently a great deal of interest is shown in the development of uranium-conserving, proliferation-resistant fuel cycle programs. These programs are intended to preserve the continuation of the present fission programs for a century or more. An important characteristic of this program is to extend the present supplies of the conventional uranium resources. These programs are predicated on the assumptions that breeders are not required in the future

1

energy scenarios and that fission alone can be treated as a long-term energy option in the planning of energy resources.

Another version of the nuclear future is to consider fusion the ultimate source of energy for the economic survival of humans. The economic feasibility of fusion is still far beyond the planning horizons of energy planners. However, the success of fusion programs becomes more promising when fusion is coupled with fission. These programs, known as fission-fusion hybrid programs, are currently being pursued at Princeton University.[1]

The research and development of alternative nuclear choices will continue in the United States as well as in other countries. A detailed and thorough understanding of uranium resources and the economics of nuclear fuel should provide a better understanding of and a rational basis for the selection of the alternative paths of nuclear programs.

Fuel Cycle Operations

Uranium mining and milling is one of the stages of the nuclear fuel cycle (figure 1-1). A first step in the fuel production process is concerned with the extraction, crushing, and leaching of the ore to extract the uranium. The product that is recovered from this process is known as yellowcake.

The recovered uranium concentrate is then converted to uranium hexafluoride, UF_6, which is then enriched to the required specification. The nat-

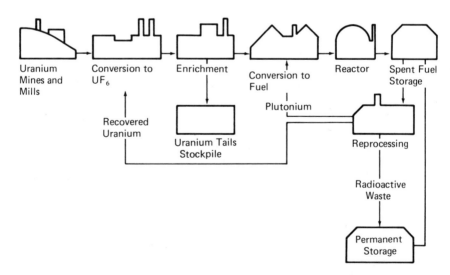

Figure 1-1. Uranium Mining and Milling in Nuclear Fuel Cycle

ural uranium contains 0.7 percent of U–235, and the uranium is then enriched in quantities of 3 to 4 percent for use in U.S. nuclear reactors. The UF_6 which is enriched to the desired requirements is then converted into uranium dioxide and finally formed into pellets. These pellets are loaded into steel tubes that are fitted with end caps. These rods are finally assembled in fixed arrays which are handled as fuel elements for reactors. After the fuel has been burned, fuel reprocessing may recover the fissile material from the waste. The radioactive wastes are the result of the various operations, including the burning of nuclear fuel, at all stages of nuclear fuel cycle. The wastes are generally classified as either high-level or low-level waste. The high-level wastes are generated from the reprocessing of nuclear reactor fuels. The management of high-level wastes requires careful planning for long-term storage. The low-level wastes are generated from chemical processing and are contained in items such as paper, metal, wood, and solid and liquid plant wastes. The radioactive wastes are transported to burial sites for permanent or temporary storage. Under the present legislation, the option of uranium recycling and reprocessing of plutonium is prohibited.[2]

Figure 1–2 is a diagram of nuclear power costs showing the complexity of and the interrelationship among the several steps in the nuclear system which account for the total electric power costs. The major components of the total cost of electric power generation are the capital, fuel, operating, and maintenance costs. Any changes within the major cost components are likely to have significant short-term as well as long-term effects on the cost of electric power production. Factors external to the electric system also influence the economics of nuclear power. Some of these factors are economic growth, population growth, regulatory and environmental constraints, and technical factors affecting the nuclear industry. Any economic forecasts of the major cost components shown in figure 1–2 should therefore consider plausible scenarios of the external factors likely to prevail in the future.

Electric Power Costs

A breakdown of nuclear electric power generation costs for a 1000–MW power plant is shown in table 1–1. The plant costs are given in 1974 dollars, and the plant is assumed to be in operation in 1982. The capital costs dominate, constituting approximately 67 percent of the total power generation costs. Interest payments during the construction period account for the highest single item of expenditure in the capital cost account. Fuel costs are relatively smaller and account for 20 percent of the total power generation costs. The uranium costs, which are of primary interest in this study, constitute 4.3 percent of the total electric power generation costs. The uranium prices, however, are a significant proportion of the total fuel costs. In table 1–1 the ratio of uranium costs to total fuel costs is calculated on the assumption that the average price of uranium

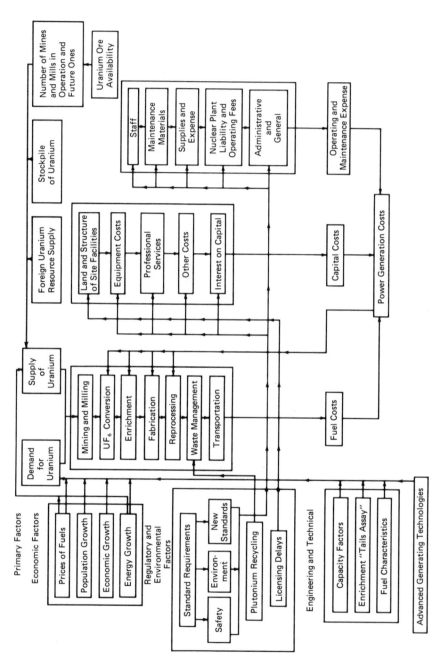

Figure 1-2. A System Flow Diagram of Nuclear Electric Power Generation Costs

Table 1-1
Breakdown of Nuclear Electric Power Generation Costs

Cost Category	Distribution of Each Cost Component (%)	Distribution of Total Generation Costs (%)
I. Capital costs[a]		
Direct costs		
Land	0.2	0.13
Structures and site facilities	11.7	7.83
Reactor or boiler equipment	17.6	11.79
Turbine plant equipment	18.4	12.32
Electric plant equipment	6.7	4.49
Miscellaneous plant equipment	1.1	0.74
Contingency and spare parts allowance	4.2	2.81
Indirect costs		
Professional services	9.2	6.16
Other costs	6.2	4.35
Interest during construction	24.4	16.38
Total capital costs	100.00	67.00
II. Fuel costs[b]		
Mining and milling	21.5	4.30
Conversion to UF_6	1.9	0.35
Enrichment	30.6	6.12
Reconversion and fabrication	7.6	1.52
Spent fuel shipping	1.1	0.22
Reprocessing	11.1	2.22
Waste management	1.4	0.28
Fuel inventory carrying charges	24.8	4.96
Total fuel costs	100.00	20.00
III. Operating and maintenance expense[c]		
Staff	70.00	9.10
Maintenance materials		
Nuclear plant liability insurance	30.00	3.90
Administrative and general		
Total operating and maintenance expense	100.00	13.00
Total costs		100.00

Note: The percent breakdown of electric power cost is calculated from the information given for a lightwater reactor of 1,000 MW capacity. The costs are given in 1974 dollars, and the electric generation costs are assumed to be 22.6 mills/kwh in 1982; see *The Nuclear Industry*, 1974, WASH-1174-74, p. 20; see also H.J. Bowers et al., "CONCEPT-Computerized Conceptual Cost Estimates for Steam Electric Power Plants," ORNL-TM-3743, April 1973.

[a]Capital costs are assumed to be $520/$KW_e$ without any escalation during construction. These costs, however, have been increasing rapidly, and appropriate changes made in the capital costs will change the distribution of costs.

[b]Fuel costs are considered in 1974 dollars (unescalated); the following unit prices were assumed in the present cost distribution: uranium $13/lb of U_3O_8 conversion to UF_6, $1.50/lb U; enrichment cost per SWU $75/kg SWU: reconversion and fabrication (no PU recycling) to be $70/kg U; spent fuel shipping $10/kg U; reprocessing as $100/kg U fuel inventory carrying charges are regarded as 15 percent of the product value.

[c]The operating and maintenance cost shows only two cost components; staff, which constitutes 70 percent of the total, includes the cost of other items not shown.

is $13 per pound. Uranium prices will increase in the future and thus escalate the nuclear fuel costs. The sensitivity of fuel costs to increasing uranium prices is important in the analysis of nuclear fuel. The economic relationship between uranium prices and power costs is simple and straightforward. For every increase of $10 in the price of uranium, the electric power generation costs are expected to increase by 1 mill per kilowatt-hour.[3] Although the power generation costs are not so sensitive to changes in uranium prices, a future price increase by a factor of ten or more can raise serious questions concerning the economic advantage of nuclear plants. The changes in uranium prices and enrichment costs are therefore significant to the utilities in the economic choice between nuclear and coal plants.

In the future coal will be the only major fuel competing with nuclear as a source of electric power production. The economic advantage of nuclear over coal electric plants has been primarily in the cost of fuel. A rapid increase in the capital costs, especially resulting from delays in construction of nuclear plants, has already made the choice between nuclear and coal a toss-up in certain parts of the country. However, nuclear continues to be economically superior in terms of its low fuel cost in the operations of electric power plants. Recent controversy concerning the adequacy of uranium reserves and resources to meet the future needs of reactors in the year 2000 has further increased the doubt and uncertainty of utility executives concerning nuclear as an economic option for electricity generation. An understanding of the future trends in the nuclear fuel costs is important to electric utilities in their decisions concerning future choices between nuclear and coal.

Notes

1. For a review of the fusion-fission hybrid reactor programs at Princeton, see F.H. Tenney, "A Brief Review of the Fusion-Fission Hybrid Reactor," Princeton Plasma Physics Laboratory, Princeton University, October 1, 1976; for references pertaining to this concept, see R.A. Huse et al., "Fusion-Fission Energy Systems: Some Utility Perspectives," Public Service Electric and Gas Company, December 3, 1974; H.A. Bethe, "The Fusion Hybrid," *Nuclear News*, 21(1978):41–44.

2. Statement by the President on Nuclear Policy, White House, October 28, 1976.

3. *Nuclear Power Issues and Choices: Report of the Nuclear Energy Policy Study Group,* Ford-Mitre, Ballinger Publishing Company, Cambridge, Mass., 1977, p. 89.

2

Uranium Industry Structure

Early Uses of Uranium

Uranium, the principal fuel for nuclear power plants, was first discovered in pitchblende in Germany in 1789. The early uses of this material were mainly of therapeutic value and led to the discovery of materials containing radium. In 1912 Colorado became the major producer; some 1,200 tons of carnotite were shipped to France, from which 8 grams of radium was extracted. A radium plant was built in Canada with a capacity of about 69,000 pounds of U_3O_8. In 1913 uranium deposits were found in the Belgian Congo, which dominated the world uranium market. Further exploratory efforts led to the discovery in 1930 of extensive uranium deposits in Canada, which then built a refinery and extracted radium. A cartel was formed between Canada and Belgium concerning the sale of radium. Other uses of uranium were confined primarily to its applications as coloring agents in ceramics and glass products and in photography. The demand for this product for these uses was estimated to be around 200 tons per year.[1]

During World War II there was a dramatic change in the use of uranium, because enormous quantities of this material were required in nuclear weapons. Large quantities were imported from the Belgian Congo, South Africa, Australia, and Portugal. From the time the Atomic Energy Commission (AEC) was formed in 1946, one of its responsibilities was to assist the domestic industry in the exploration and discovery of uranium deposits in the United States and Canada.[2]

The Atomic Energy Act of 1954 provided the AEC with the responsibility for maintaining a viable domestic uranium industry. The Private Ownership of Special Nuclear Material Act of 1964 allowed the AEC to enter into contracts with private industry for uranium enrichment. This decision gave the uranium-mining industry the first opportunity to sell the uranium in the commercial market.

The AEC's sole procurement of uranium ended in 1968, allowing the participation of private industry until 1970. Since 1970, uranium has been bought and sold by private firms. Of all the operations necessary to convert uranium ore into a finished fabricated material as a fuel for use in nuclear plants, the enrichment operations are the only ones owned wholly by the government. The current intention of the U.S. Department of Energy is to allow additional enrichment capacity to be operated in the private industry sector. The prices of various services performed in the nuclear fuel cycle will there-

7

fore be determined in the private markets by the interactions of the forces of supply and demand.

Market Structure

The economic phases of uranium mining and milling operations can be studied under three different ownerships which form a link in exploration, mining, and milling of uranium. The three stages of operations are owned and operated by different industries of varying sizes, which all have a common goal of maximizing the return on investment. The industry type, concentration level, and capital intensity of the operations provide information on the relative ease of entry, degree of effective competition, and the supply and price of the uranium-mining operations. This section examines some of the salient features of this emerging industry to determine the future outlook of the uranium-mining industry.

In the early phase of the uranium industry the AEC was the sole agent for the exploration of the low-cost uranium reserves. The purpose of the AEC in entering this business was to develop a commercial market for the uranium industry. The history of uranium exploration has an interesting pattern of change in ownership. Large oil companies and small firms entered and left the industry from time to time as conditions were found to be attractive.[3] In recent years the electric utilities have been active in the uranium exploratory ventures. The role of the utilities in the uranium exploration will become more and more prominent as they try to procure assured uranium supplies for power plants.

As of 1971 seven large companies held 70 percent of the low-cost uranium reserves ($8 per pound), while ten other companies had control of 20 percent of the reserves. A total of seventeen companies held 90 percent of the total uranium reserves in 1971.[4] This situation changed slightly in 1975, when eight companies were reported to have owned 75 percent of the reserves and twenty-five firms held 95 percent of the total reserves.[5] In recent years there has been a great deal of concern about the existence of a possible uranium cartel. Table 2–1 provides the recent breakdown of domestic reserve holdings by different companies. Kerr-McGee holds the largest amount of U.S. uranium reserves, followed by Gulf Oil Company. The reserve holdings are also ranked to show the importance of each company in uranium mining and milling. The concentration ratios for uranium reserve holdings suggest a possibility of oligopolistic pricing behavior, especially when compared with coal, which is a competing fuel for electricity production (table 2–2). But when the uranium industry is compared with other industries, such as copper and aluminum, the concentration ratios in uranium reserves holdings are not high enough to warrant legislation for possible violation of antitrust laws.[6] However, there has been a great deal of interest concerning the involvement of oil companies, which may necessitate some legis-

Table 2-1
U.S. Uranium Reserve Holdings, Concentrate Production, and Milling Operations

	U.S. Uranium Reserves Holdings (1976)			U.S. U_3O_8 Concentrate Production of Uranium Milling Companies (1975)			U.S. Uranium Milling Capacity (1976)		
	Rank[a]	Percentage of Total	Reserves (Thousands of Tons)[b]	Rank[a]	Percentage of Total	U_3O_8 Concentrate Production (Tons)	Rank[a]	Percentage of Total	Milling Capacity (Tons of Ore Per Day)
Kerr-McGee	1	21.0	145	1	15.8	1,800	1	24.6	7,000
Gulf Oil	2	11.6	80	—	—	—	—	—	—
United Nuclear	3	5.8	40	6	6.8	775	2	12.3	3,500
Continental Oil	4	3.6	25	9	4.2	481	7	6.2	1,750
Western Nuclear	5	3.3	22.5		NA	NA	8	4.2	1,200
Getty Oil	6	2.9	20		NA	NA			
Utah International	7	2.5	17.5	2	15.3	1,750	4	10.5	3,000
Exxon	8	2.5	17.5	5	7.4	850	5	10.5	3,000
Anaconda	9	2.2	15.0	3	15.1	1,700	3	10.5	3,000
Phillips Petroleum	10	1.8	12.5	7	5.1	600	11	2.5	700
Rio Algom Mines	11	1.3	9.0						
Reserve Oil & Mineral	12	0.8	5.5						
Union Pacific	13	0.7	5.0						
Sohio	14	0.7	5.0	4	8.7	1,000	6	8.8	2,500
Union Carbide	15	0.6	4.0	12	2.8	324			
Pioneer Corporation	16	0.6	4.0	8	4.2	484	9	3.5	1,000
Atlas	17	0.4	3.0						
Socal	18	0.4	3.0						
Ranchers Exploration	19	0.3	3.0						
Houston Natural Gas	20	0.2	1.5						
Federal Reserve	21	0.2	1.5		NA	NA	10	3.3	950

(continued)

Table 2-1 continued

	U.S. Uranium Reserves Holdings (1976)			U.S. U_3O_8 Concentrate Production of Uranium Milling Companies (1975)			U.S. Uranium Milling Capacity (1976)		
	Rank[a]	Percentage of Total	Reserves (Thousands of Tons)[b]	Rank[a]	Percentage of Total	U_3O_8 Concentrate Production (Tons)	Rank[a]	Percentage of Total	Milling Capacity (Tons of Ore Per Day)
American Nuclear	22	0.1	1.0						
Cotter Corporation (Commonwealth Edison)				10	3.5	400	12	1.6	450
Dawn (Newmont)				11	3.0	345	13	1.4	400
Homestake Mining Company				13	1.7	194			

Source: *Petroleum Industry Involvement in Alternative Source of Energy*, committee on Energy and Natural Resources, U.S. Senate, 95th Congress, 1st Sess., September 1977, pp. 326, 327, 330.

[a]Rank identifies the importance of each of these companies in the uranium-mining industry.

[b]Total U.S. reserves are for the price $30/lb of U_3O_8.

Table 2-2
Concentration Ratios for Uranium and Coal Reserve Holdings

	Uranium Reserves Holdings (1976)	Coal Reserves Holdings (1975)
Four-firm total	42	26
Eight-firm total	53	36
Fifteen-firm total	61	46

Source: *Petroleum Industry Involvement in Alternative Sources of Energy,* Committee on Energy and Natural Resources, U.S. Senate, 95th Congress, 1st Sess., September 1977, pp. 283, 326.

lative measures for the horizontal divestiture of petroleum industry. As of 1976 oil companies held 47 percent of the uranium reserves in the United States.

Another view discounts the possibility of undue influence of oil companies in the uranium industry. Nininger claims that the total reserve holdings by the top ten companies have declined since 1966. The large companies with significant reserve holdings left the industry in 1966, while seventeen new companies entered the uranium market. In 1966 four of the ten top companies were the oil companies. The relative share of oil companies increased to five of the ten companies in 1975. Nininger points out that this change cannot be characterized as takeover by petroleum industry.[7]

On the basis of historical information, one can state that the entry into the uranium exploration and reserve holdings is relatively easy and is not precluded by the concentration of production and assets of a few firms. The degree of risk as perceived by the firms, in terms of the uncertainty of future demand for uranium, determines the rate of expansion and future characteristics of this phase of uranium industry operations.

Another aspect of the uranium industry is the control over mining and milling operations. It appears that a large number of mining companies acquire ownership in the milling operations. Many of the top ten companies that control uranium reserves also rank high in the production of uranium concentrate and the uranium-milling capacity (table 2-1). In the case of milling there appears to be a relatively higher level of concentration when compared with the uranium concentrate production and reserve holdings of the uranium industry. However, it is difficult to analyze the mining and milling operations separately because in many cases they are intertwined in terms of interest, ownership, and economics of the operations. Though concentration in mill ownership has declined from 1955 to 1970, the ownership of more than 50 percent of capacity has always remained in the hands of four firms in the industry (table 2-3).

A recent survey by the U.S. Department of Energy shows that as of September 1977 twenty-three milling companies had an operating capacity of 34,680 tons of ore per day (table 2-4). Many more mills have announced their

Table 2-3
Concentration in Mill Ownership

Year	Concentration Level (Percent of Total Mill Production)			Number of Mills
	4 Firms	8 Firms	20 Firms	
1955	79.8	99.1	100.0	9
1960	51.4	72.4	99.6	25
1965	55.4	79.3	100.0	20
1970	55.3	80.0	100.0	16

Source: Electric Power Research Institute, *Uranium Price Formation,* Charles River Associates, Report EA-498, pp. 8-40.

intention to enter the milling operations; their entrance would increase the future milling capacity to 51,000 tons of ore per day.

A brief review of the literature on the uranium exploration, mining, and milling operations shows that entry is easy, the capital requirements are not so enormous, and the technology is simple; entry is therefore accessible to all willing entrants. However, the necessity of acquiring large blocks of lands may be a barrier to entry by small firms. The survey of industry ownership reveals that a few large firms may control the supply and the price of uranium. There is a definite trend for oil companies to be involved in the uranium mining and milling industry. It is beyond the scope of this work to support or refute the existence of a uranium cartel. An investigation has been underway to determine whether there is a lack of competition, thus violating antitrust laws in the coal, gas, and uranium industries. If a uranium cartel is a fact, and if policies are designed to control the supply and thus increase the price, the consequences of such actions will be adverse to the nuclear economy. Leontief once stated a proverb about "a gypsy who decided to train his horse not to eat which was very good. He was a poor gypsy; he ate the food himself. And he practically trained it, but accidentally, the horse died."[8] Likewise, a uranium cartel's attempt to control supply in order to reap abnormal profits could become a serious obstacle to the growth of nuclear, and in the long run this attempt would invite government intervention in controlling the supply and prices of uranium. This work assumes that a uranium cartel does not exist and that any such cartel would be broken up by the federal government in order to restore the competitive pressures of the market economy.

In this study the future supplies, demand, and prices of uranium from 1975 to 2000 are examined on the premise that the future demand and supply responds primarily to the market price without any outside intervention or control.

Table 2-4
Uranium-Milling Companies and Plants, Location and Capacity, 1977

Mills Operating	Plant Location	Nominal Capacity (Tons Ore per Day)	Percentage of Capacity
Anaconda Company[a]	Grants, New Mexico	2,500	7.21
Atlas Corporation	Moab, Utah	1,100	3.17
Continental Oil Company–Pioneer Nuclear, Inc.[b]	Falls City, Texas	1,750	5.04
Cotter (Commonwealth Edison)[c]	Canon City, Colorado	450	1.30
Dawn Mining Company	Ford, Washington	400	1.15
Exxon Company	Powder River Basin, Wyoming	3,000	8.65
Federal-American[d]	Gas Hills, Wyoming	950	2.74
Intercontinental Energy Corporation	Pawnee, Texas	_[e]	–
Kerr-McGee Nuclear Corp.	Grants, New Mexico	7,000	20.25
Lucky Mc Uranium Corp.	Gas Hills, Wyoming	1,650	4.76
Lucky Mc Uranium Corp.	Sherley Basin, Wyoming	1,800	5.19
Mobil Oil Company	Bruni, Texas	_[e]	–
Rio Algom Corporation	La Sal, Utah	700	2.02
Rocky Mountain Energy and Mono Power[f]	Powder River Basin, Wyoming	1,000	2.88
Sohio Oil, Reserve Oil and Minerals	Cebolleta, New Mexico	1,660	4.79
Union Carbide Corporation	Uravan, Colorado	1,300	3.75
Union Carbide Corporation	Natrona County, Wyoming	1,200	3.46
United Nuclear Corporation	Church Rock, New Mexico	3,000	8.65
United Nuclear-Homestake Partners	Grants, New Mexico	3,500	10.09
U.S. Steel	George West, Texas	_[e]	–
U.S. Steel-Niagara Mohawk	George West, Texas	_[e]	–
Uranium Recovery Corp. (UNC)	Mulberry, Florida	_[g]	–
Western Nuclear, Inc.	Jeffrey City, Wyoming	1,700	4.90
Total operating		34,660	100.00
Mills Currently Inoperative			
Getty Oil Company	Shirley Basin, Wyoming	1,750	77.77
Tennessee Valley Authority	Edgemont, S. Dakota	500	22.23
Total inoperative		2,250	100.00
Mills under Construction			
Freeport Uranium Recovery Corporation	Uncle Sam, Louisiana	_[g]	–
Western Nuclear Corp.	Wellpinit, Washington	2,000	100.00
Wyoming Mineral (Westinghouse)	Bruni, Texas	_[a]	–
Wyoming Mineral	Ray Point, Texas	_[a]	–
Wyoming Mineral	Bingham Canyon, Utah	_[h]	–
Wyoming Mineral Corp.	Pierce, Florida	_[g]	–
Total under construction		2,000	100.00

Table 2–4 continued

Mills Operating	Plant Location	Nominal Capacity (Tons Ore per Day)	Percentage of Capacity
Mills Announced			
Chevron (Standard of California)	Panna Maria, Texas	2,000	16.53
Gardinier, Inc.	Tampa, Florida	_g	–
Homestake Mining	Marshall Pass, Colorado	600	4.96
Kerr-McGee Nuclear Corp.	Powder River Basin, Wyoming	2,000	16.53
Phillips Petroleum Co.	Nose Rock, New Mexico	2,500	20.66
Ranchers Exploration & Devel.	Naturita, Colorado	_i	–
Solution Engineering	Falls City, Texas	_i	–
Union Oil Company (Minerals Exploration Company)	Red Desert, Wyoming	3,000	24.79
United Nuclear Corporation	Powder River Basin, Wyoming	2,000	16.53
Total announced		12,100	100.00
Total operating, inoperative, under construction, and announced		51,010	

Source: Raw Materials, Supply Evaluation Branch, Department of Energy, September 30, 1977.
[a]Being expanded to 6,000 tons per day
[b]Being expanded to 2,900 tons per day
[c]Being expanded to 1,000 tons per day
[d]To be expanded to 3,000 tons per day
[e]Solution mining methods
[f]Southern California Edison and Union Pacific Railroad
[g]Recovery from phosphoric acid
[h]Recovery from copper dump leach liquor
[i]Heap leach tailings

Future Patterns of Industry

It is not difficult to portray the future pattern of industry if the firms expand their operations to produce uranium from nonconventional sources. Such a situation is likely to arise if the nuclear fission programs continue to be the mainstay of the energy economy well beyond the present century and the uranium requirements far exceed the availability of uranium from conventional sandstone deposits. Under the assumption that uranium is extracted from such nonconventional sources as shale and seawater, the uranium markets can be characterized as highly risky, and only firms with large capital bases can afford to enter the uranium market. To mitigate the high risk involved in the capital-intensive uranium extraction projects, the government may even have to provide som economic incentives or subsidies, as has been proposed in the case of enrichment operations. The economics of nonconventional resource utilization is not within the scope of this study, because the analysis extends only to the end of this century.

Another distinguishing characteristic of the future of the uranium market will be the diversity of ownership as more uranium is derived as a by-product of the phosphoric acid, copper-leach operations and from the residue of coal and lignite power plants and gasification plants. The economic relationship will be more analogous to oil and gas production in the United States over a period of time. The future trends in the industry will be determined mainly by the growth in nuclear power, reactor technology, and the cumulative requirements of uranium.

Notes

1. U.S. Department of the Interior, *Bureau of Mines, Mineral Facts and Problems,* Bulletin 650, 1970, pp. 221–222; Energy Research and Development Administration, *U.S. Nuclear Power Export Activities,* ERDA-1542, vol. 1, April 1976, pp. 3–37.

2. ERDA, *U.S. Nuclear Power Export Activities,* pp 3–37; U.S. Atomic Energy Commission, *Fourth Semi-Annual Report,* January–June 1948.

3. Electric Power Research Institute, *Uranium Price Formation,* prepared by the Charles River Associates, Report EA-498, October 1977; section 8 of this report provides an interesting historical background of the uranium market structure since the beginning of the uranium mining and milling industry.

4. Ibid., pp. 8–21.

5. D. Sanders, "The Price of Energy," in *Competition in the U.S. Energy Industry,* A Report to the Energy Policy Project of the Ford Foundation, ed. T.D. Duchesneau, Ballinger Publishing Company, Cambridge, Mass., 1975, p. 401.

6. Four-firm ratios for copper and aluminum are said to be as high as 72 and 79; see C.R. McConnell, *Economics,* 7th ed., McGraw-Hill, New York, 1978, pp. 592–610.

7. R.D. Nininger, "Uranium Resources and Supply," *Atomic Industrial Forum: Fuel Cycle, 1977,* April 24, 1977, pp. 13–14.

8. W. Leontief, "Models and Decisions," in *Mineral Materials Modeling,* ed. W.A. Vogley, Johns Hopkins University Press, Baltimore, Md., 1975, p. 56.

3 U.S. Uranium Reserves and Resources

The availability of a natural resource is primarily a function of technology and price. The supply of a resource is generally expressed in terms of its price for a given level of technology. The higher the prices, the higher the amounts of resource that will be supplied by the producers. Technological progress in the exploration and development generally augments the resource base.

A quantitative description of uranium reserves and resources is generally given in terms of the types of the deposits—sandstone, vein, lignite, and conglomerate. The largest uranium source found in the United States is in the sandstone deposits of Colorado, Utah, New Mexico, Wyoming, and South Dakota. Uranium was deposited within the rock formation as a result of the circulation of ground water, and the size of the deposit and the amount of ore present varies from deposit to deposit. Similarly the grade of the deposit mined varies from 0.1 percent to 0.5 percent of U_3O_8. The next important uranium sources are vein deposits, which were formed along fractures in various kinds of rocks by deposition from circulating igneous fluids. The extraction of uranium from these deposits requires the separation of the chemicals associated with it.[1]

Definition of Reserves and Resource

The Grand Junction Office of the Energy Research and Development Administration (ERDA) compiles and publishes annually comprehensive statistical information concerning the various resource aspects of the uranium industry.[2] The statistical information given in the uranium industry report is based on information furnished voluntarily by the uranium exploration, mining, and milling companies. The statistical information on uranium resource availability is reported as reserves and potential resources. The term *reserves* denotes the quantity of uranium that can be economically recovered from the known deposits within the specified scope of costs. In the definition of reserves, the quantity, grade, and physical characteristics of the ore will have been established with reasonable certainty on the basis of present technology and scientific knowledge. The term *potential resource* is the quantity of uranium that is estimated to exist in unexplored areas of the country or in extensions of the known deposits. These estimates are made on the basis of well-known geologic principles and extrapolations from explored to unexplored areas.

The estimates of ore reserves and potential resources are revised from time

17

to time on the basis of geologic information and new discoveries. The interrelationship between uranium resources, uranium costs, and the knowledge of its availability is illustrated in figure 3-1. Read downward, the reserves and potential resource in figure 3-1 show the increasing availability of uranium resources, at higher cost per pound of U_3O_8, as a decreasing function of reliability. Similarly the reliability of resource availability decreases as one moves from the uranium reserves category to different categories of uranium resource potential. The last column, headed "Unassessed" is left to be filled by geologists and economists for assessing the uranium availability as a function of technology and various other factors that affect the knowledge of resource availability.

The uranium reserve and resource estimates are provided by the Department of Energy (DOE) on the basis of the forward costs per pound of U_3O_8. Forward costs are those that have not been incurred in connection with current uranium mining. The possibility of confusion in the understanding of ore reserves and resources in terms of forward cost has been pointed out in the report prepared by the National Academy of Sciences.[3] The study suggests that the reserves and resource classification should be made on the basis of the concentration of uranium rather than on a monetary basis which changes from time to time.

It is helpful to know how these cost estimates are made. Forward costs are the future capital and operating costs of mine development and operation; they do not include profit and sunk costs, which comprise expenditures for property acquisition, exploration, and mine development. The procedure used by the

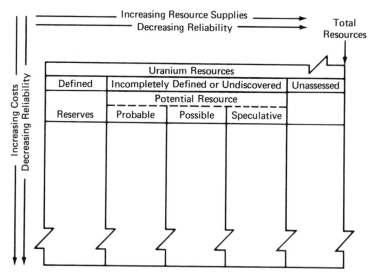

Figure 3-1. A Schematic View of Uranium Reserves and Resources

Department of Energy in estimating the ore reserves for different forward cost categories is briefly described here. The cutoff point of ore grade for a given forward cost category is determined on the basis of the lowest grade of material that can be mined at a minimum thickness, where the total operating cost per pound of recoverable U_3O_8 is equal to the chosen maximum forward cost per pound.[4] The cutoff grade is calculated as follows.

$$\text{Cutoff grade (lowest grade in percent of } U_3O_8) = \frac{\text{Cost of mining, hauling, royalty, and milling}}{\text{Maximum forward cost per pound of } U_3O_8 \times \text{mill recovery} \times 20}$$

An example of the calculation of the cutoff grade is given for the forward cost category of $10 per pound of U_3O_8. Assume that the total operating cost is broken down as follows.

Cost Item	Dollars per Ton
Direct mining	9.00
Indirect mining	0.50
Haulage	2.50
Royalty	3.00
Milling	5.00
Total operating cost	20.00

By knowing the total operating cost and the maximum forward cost of uranium, in this case $10 per pound of U_3O_8, one can calculate the minimum cutoff grade.

$$\text{Minimum cutoff grade} = \frac{\text{Total operating cost}}{\text{Maximum forward cost} \times \text{mill recovery} \times 20}$$

$$= \frac{20}{10 \times 0.94 \times 20}$$

$$= 0.11 \text{ percent } U_3O_8$$

Similarly the cutoff grades for various forward cost categories can be calculated by substituting the desired maximum forward costs in the general formula. Suppose that a sample of ore that is estimated to have an average grade of 0.30 percent U_3O_8 is evaluated for inclusion as reserve in one of the forward cost categories. The average grade of the sample is then used to determine the operating cost per pound of U_3O_8.

$$\frac{\text{Operating cost}}{\text{per pound of } U_3 O_8} = \frac{\text{Total operating costs}}{\text{Ore grade of the sample} \times 20}$$

$$= \frac{\$20.00}{0.30 \text{ percent} \times 20}$$

$$= \$3.33$$

The Department of Energy then calculates the forward capital costs, which include the expenditures on mine design, surface plant and equipment, and mine development. If the capital cost per pound of $U_3 O_8$ is \$1.00, the forward cost in this case is estimated to be \$4.33 per pound of $U_3 O_8$. The difference between the estimated forward cost and the maximum forward cost is said to allow the recovery of the past cost and the cost of money that has not been included in the mining and milling of the selected ore.[5] The forward costs are different from the economic costs; they do not include the return on capital and the taxes on producers' earnings. The economic costs of uranium reserves are higher than the forward costs because they include the opportunity cost of capital. For a 15 percent after-tax rate of return, a recent study has estimated the ratio between economic and forward costs to be 1.4 to 1 for the reserves in production and 1.7 to 1 for reserves not in production. In the derivation of long-run uranium supply this study assumes the ratio of economic costs of extraction to the forward cost of extraction to be 2 to 1.[6]

One should keep in mind that the increases in cost reflected by inflationary pressures decrease the amount of reserves shown in one category but increase the amount in the higher-cost category. This process does not indicate a reduction in the amount of ore present. Because of the changes in monetary accounting, the \$8 reserves no longer exist as shown in the 1976 record; they were changed to \$10 reserves in 1977. This gradual upward trend in the cost category of the ore grade is likely to continue. This change will also have an effect in showing the additional higher-cost category of uranium in the accounting of U.S. uranium reserves. A simple relationship between the forward costs and ore grade as reported by the Department of Energy is shown in figure 3-2. The inflationary effect simply pushes the curve upward over a period of time.

U.S. Reserve Statistics

There have been continual revisions in the reserve estimates of different cost categories from 1965 to 1977 as reported by the Department of Energy (table 3-1). The estimated reserves in the cost category of \$10 per pound have decreased from 315 to 250 thousand tons of uranium from 1975 to 1977. This

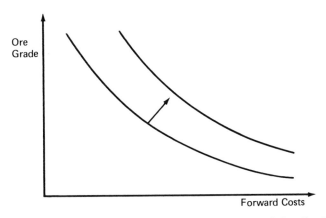

Figure 3-2. Relationship between Forward Costs and Ore Grade

decrease should be viewed as a transfer of physical resource to a higher-cost category component rather than total actual depletion of this reserve category. The $50 cost category has been added recently, and the trend toward the addition of higher-cost categories is likely to continue as inflationary pressures push the production costs upward and as the need for increasing amounts of uranium is felt. In the future, as more and more of uranium is produced, the uranium reserves in the lower-cost category will diminish and finally disappear as higher-cost uranium appears in the accounting of uranium reserves. The current estimates of uranium reserves and resources are in the amount of 4.17 million tons, as shown in table 3-2. Of the total, 840 thousand tons of U_3O_8 can be produced at a forward cost of $50 or less per pound of U_3O_8. From the information shown in table 3-2, the uranium reserve-supply for different levels

Table 3-1
Revision of Reserves, 1965-1977

| | Thousands of Tons of U_3O_8 | | | |
Year	$10/lb	$15/lb	$30/lb	$50/lb
1965	175	–	–	–
1970	250	317	–	–
1975	315	420	600	–
1976	270	430	640	–
1977	250	410	680	840

Source: Energy Research and Development Administration, *Statistical Data of the Uranium Industry,* Grand Junction Office, Report GJO-100 (1977), Grand Junction, Colorado, p. 26.

Table 3-2
U.S. Uranium Ore Reserves and Resources as of January 1, 1977
(thousands of tons of U_3O_8)

Cutoff Cost (Dollars per Pound of U_3O_8)	Average Grade (%)	Reserves of U_3O_8[a]	Potential Resource of U_3O_8		
			Probable[b]	Possible[c]	Speculative[d]
10	0.19	250	275	115	100
15	0.14	410	585	490	190
30	0.09	680	1,090	1,120	480
50	0.07	840	1,370	1,420	540

Source: Energy Research and Development Administration, *Statistical Data of the Uranium Industry,* Grand Junction Office Report GJO-100, Grand Junction, Colorado, pp. 26, 43.

[a]Approximately 140,000 tons of U_3O_8 recoverable as a by-product of phosphate and copper production during 1975-2000 may also be included.

[b]Probable potential resources are those estimated to occur in known uranium districts and are further postulated to be in (1) extensions of known deposits, (2) new deposits within trends or areas of mineralization, and (3) deposits that have been identified by exploration.

[c]Possible potential resources are those estimated to occur in new deposits in formations or productive geologic settings elsewhere (1) within the same geologic province or subprovince under similar geologic conditions or (2) within the same geologic province or subprovince under different geologic conditions.

[d]Speculative potential resources are those estimated to occur in new deposits (1) in formations or geologic settings not previously productive within a productive geologic province or subprovince or (2) within a geologic province or subprovince not previously productive.

of cutoff costs is presented in table 3-3. The reserve-supply of different levels of cutoff costs is useful in characterizing the possible alternative paths of reserve and resource depletion over a period of time. Many depletion schemes can be identified in relation to the sequence in which the resources are converted into reserves to supply uranium production. Path I shown in figure 3-3 illustrates the production trend from low-cost reserves to higher-costs reserves. The potential resources of different categories are converted into reserves and are then depleted in a downward movement from low-cost to high-cost uranium categories. In this case the decline in ore grade will be rapid and sudden as a cumulative quantity of uranium produced is increased. In path II the producers deplete the reserves and resources in a horizontal manner for each cost category. The ore grade decline will be gradual in this case. Path III represents a strategy that is more likely to be used by the producers in the depletion of resources. The relationships between the cumulative quantity of uranium produced and the ore grade provide useful information in determining the most likely range of production costs in the supply of uranium production. The characterization of the different trends in the supply of uranium reserves and production will also provide

Table 3-3
Reserve-Supply for Different Levels of Average Cutoff Cost

Cutoff Costs ($)	Average Cutoff Cost ($)	Reserves	Resources	Total
			(Thousands of Tons of U_3O_8)	
10	5	250	490	740
10–15	12	160	775	935
15–30	23	270	1,425	1,695
30–50	40	160	640	800

a basis for the derivation of long-run incremental costs as a function of quantity produced.

A review of the uranium reserves and resources indicates that the United States has a sufficient resource base of conventional sandstone deposits to meet the needs of projected maximum nuclear capacity to the year 2000. This study is therefore concerned with the economic analysis of uranium reserves and resources as estimated by the Department of Energy in table 3-2. The study is confined to the industry behavior in the conversion into reserves of uranium resources of $50 per pound or less and the effects of the level of reserves on the supply of uranium production and on price formation.

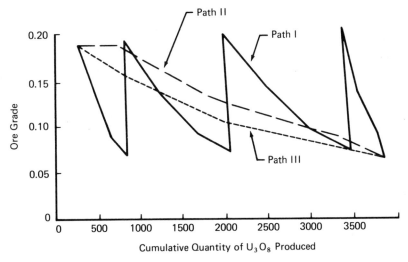

Figure 3-3. Alternative Uranium Depletion Schemes and Ore Grade

Reserves and Addition to Reserves

An understanding of the uranium ore reserves situation requires a careful study of the historical factors affecting the activities relating to drilling and production of ore. The uranium reserves (RR) at any given year can be expressed as

$$
\begin{aligned}
RR_t = \Sigma RR_{it} = \{ & [RR_{1t-1} + FR_{1t} \pm RS_{1t} - q_{1t}^s] \\
& + [RR_{2t-1} + FR_{2t} \pm RS_{2t} - q_{2t}^s] \\
& + [RR_{3t-1} + FR_{3t} \pm RS_{3t} - q_{3t}^s] \quad (3.1) \\
& + [RS_{4t-1} + FR_{4t} \pm RS_{4t} - q_{4t}^s] \}
\end{aligned}
$$

$$
i = 1, 2, 3, 4
$$

where

1   indicates reserves at less than \$10 per lb

2   indicates reserves at \$10–\$15 per lb

3   indicates reserves at \$15–\$30 per lb

4   indicates reserves at \$30 per lb and over

FR represents new discoveries

RS represents revisions

q^s represents quantity produced

The new discoveries of uranium (FR) are the result of exploratory drilling. The revisions of resources (RS) occur mainly because of the increased drilling efforts that accompany the development of resource deposits. Information concerning the changes in uranium ore reserves due to reevaluation, additions, and subtractions is not available for the period beginning 1948 in detail comparable to the ore reserve statistics, except for the last few years.

In this study the term *addition to reserves* includes the new findings as well as the changes in the reserves due to revisions. The addition to reserves, ΔRR, is calculated as

$$
RR_t = RR_{t-1} + \Delta RR_t - q_t^s \quad (3.2)
$$

or

$$
\Delta RR_t = RR_t - (RR_{t-1} - q_t^s) \quad (3.3)
$$

The historical time series data for $10 reserves are available for the period 1947–1977. The higher cost reserves, $15, $30, and $50, were added in recent years.

An important aspect of reserve analysis in this section is to establish a relationship that explains the factors affecting the level of uranium reserves. Some of the important factors are exploratory drilling, development drilling, number of holes drilled, and the rate of uranium discovery.

Various measures have been suggested for studying the relationship between uranium resource and drilling effort.[7] A commonly used measure is the discovery rate, which is defined to be the pounds of uranium discovered per foot drilled. The drilling effort used in the calculation of discovery rate can be exploratory, development, or total surface and underground drilling. The measure, discovery rate, depends on the depth of holes drilled. Very high discovery rates were observed during the years 1954–1957, reporting a discovery of fourteen pounds of uranium per foot drilled. However, this trend has not continued, and the average discovery rate has been falling over a period of time. It has been the practice in the uranium-mining industry to consider the average discovery rate to be two pounds per foot drilled.[8] The usefulness of the discovery rate as an index in the analysis and forecasts of uranium supply has been seriously questioned. The discovery rate reflects results that are heavily biased toward the exploration results reported from the geological and production centers within the local vicinity. Another measure of uranium discovery is tons per hole, which is independent of the depth of holes drilled. However, this measure suffers from the same deficiencies as pounds per foot drilled in the representation of the success of exploration effort.

After evaluating the merits and the limitations of the effort-yield indices, this study considered a set of relationships that seem appropriate in the forecasting of the long-term trends in additions to uranium reserves. In the specification of the relationships, the effect of drilling as well as the number of holes drilled were considered important variables in explaining the long-term behavior of additions to reserves. The following equation was then selected for estimation and model simulation.

$$\log \Delta RR_t = \alpha + \beta_1 \log CDR_{t-1} + \beta_2 \log DND_{t-1} \qquad (3.4)$$

where

ΔRR = addition to reserves of $10 and higher-cost category (thousand tons of U_3O_8)

CDR = cumulative drilling, including exploratory and development (million feet)

DND = total number of holes drilled (exploratory and development)

Equation 3.4 emphasizes the importance of cumulative drilling as well as the number of holes drilled. In the overall development of the model, it was felt that both the exploratory and the development drilling should be the explanatory variables. Therefore the cumulative drilling and the number of holes drilled were selected to reflect the total drilling activity.

An alternate formulation of the addition to reserves relates to the exploratory drilling and the number of exploratory holes drilled.

$$\log \Delta RR_t = \alpha + \beta_1 \log EXD_{t-1} + \beta_2 \log NDE_{t-1} \qquad (3.4a)$$

where

EXD = exploratory drilling (million feet)

NDE = number of exploratory holes drilled

Equation 3.4a was estimated but not included in the model simulation. In both equations the drilling and the holes drilled are shown with a lag, since the effects of drilling activities are compiled and shown after a year or so. A recent study on uranium analysis suggests that the total reserves discovered be related to the level of reserves discovered in the previous year, cost of uranium extraction, and the time trend.[9]

$$RD_{pt} = e^{\alpha_0 + \alpha_1 T} RD_{pt-1}^{\alpha_2} D^{\alpha_3} P^{\alpha_4}$$

where

RD_{pt} = reserves of uranium discovered with extraction cost of less than p

D = exploratory and development drilling

P = marginal cost of extraction

T = time in years

This formulation seems credible in estimating the long-term trends in addition to reserves for the purpose of developing uranium supply curve. However, the inclusion of price in explaining the level of reserves is somewhat questionable. The price, as seen in the present analysis, affects the drilling activity, which in turn determines the level of uranium discovered.

Notes

1. National Academy of Sciences, *Mineral Resources and the Environment. Supplementary Report: Reserves and Resources of Uranium in the United States,* Washington, D.C., 1975.

2. Energy Research and Development Administration, *Statistical Data of the Uranium Industry,* Grand Junction Office Report GJO-100, Grand Junction, Colorado, January 1, 1977.

3. NAS, *Mineral Resources and the Environment,* p. 12. A study on uranium data points out that several measures that can be incorporated in the reporting of the uranium statistical data would increase the reliability of statistical and economic analysis (Electric Power Research Institute, *Uranium Data,* EPRI, EA-400, 1977).

4. ERDA, *Statistical Data,* p. 22.

5. R.J. Meeham, "Ore Reserves," Resource Division, Grand Junction Office, U.S. Department of Energy, pp. 23-25.

6. Lewis J. Pearl, "The GESMO Utility Group on U_3O_8 Prices," testimony before the Generic and Environmental Statement on Mixed Oxide Fuel (GESMO) Hearing Board, U.S. Nuclear Regulatory Commission, April 14, 1977, pp. 14, 15.

7. R.T. Zitting, "Estimation of Potential Uranium Resource," in *Mineral Resources and the Environment,* p. 148.

8. Electric Power Research Institute, *Uranium Price Formation,* prepared by the Charles River Associates, Report EA-498, October 1977, pp. 5-52.

9. Pearl, "GESMO Utility Group," p. 16.

4

Alternative Estimates of Resources

In recent years a great deal has been written about uranium resource estimation, especially about the adequacy of uranium to meet the future energy needs of the U.S. economy. Depending on the interests and background of the resource analysts, different analytic approaches have been used in the modeling of resource assessment.[1] Because of the differences in the quantitative approaches and the assumptions incorporated in the modeling of the uranium industry, the estimates of the availability of conventional uranium resources cover a wide range. The conservative estimates, which point out the limited resource base, have generated controversy over the physical depletion of the resource well before the end of this century. Estimates on the lower side have also created some doubt about the reliability of the method used by the Department of Energy in the appraisal of uranium resource and the use of this information by others in the analysis of energy alternatives. This chapter briefly reviews different studies dealing with conventional as well as nonconventional sources of uranium for the United States.

Some Optimistic Views

In 1975 Searl and Platt reviewed the studies and methodologies used in the estimation of uranium and thorium resources of the United States.[2] Using the existing information on exploration, reserve, and production data, the authors applied the geoeconomic approach in the derivation of additional information concerning the physical distribution of uranium. The Energy Research and Development Administration (ERDA) postulates that low-cost uranium, $10 per pound, can be found at a depth of 4,000 feet. On this basis ERDA estimates of low-cost uranium reserves that were reported at a depth of 400 feet were increased by a factor of ten; likewise the availability of potential resource was also raised. The uranium resource estimates were made for the known producing areas as well as for the nonproducing areas of the United States, which includes the areas of Alaska, the eastern states, and the other areas of the western part of the United States. The cost estimates, which include discovery, recovery, and milling, were said to be less than $100 per pound of U_3O_8. An underlying principle of this approach is that "all resource estimates, whether accompanied by subjective probabilities or not, contain a strong element of judgment and therefore are subjective in nature. Consequently, it appears that a resource estimate conveys much more meaningful information if such probabilities are attached to the resource estimates."[3] The estimated availability of conventional deposits of uranium as a function of subjective probability is shown in figure 4-1. More than 30 million tons of U_3O_8 can be produced at a cost of less than $100 per pound, with a subjective probability of 3 to 4 percent. However, one cannot formulate any long-term nuclear plans on the basis of such a low subjective probability of uranium resource availability. Furthermore, uranium on the order of 25 million to 30 million tons may not be available, since environmental and social factors will constrain uranium production. A realistic appraisal of resource availability, according to this study, is that 6 million tons of uranium can be recovered at $100 per pound from the known production districts with a subjective probability of 50 percent. The estimates of Searl and Platt, which are relatively optimistic with regard to the availabil-

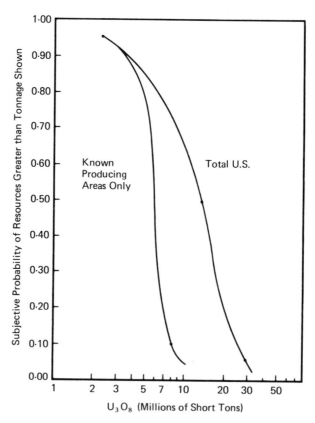

Source: Reprinted with permission from *Annals of Nuclear Energy,* vol. 2., p. 759, M.F. Searl and J. Platt, "Views on Uranium and Thorium Resources," © May 1975, Pergaman Press, Ltd.

Figure 4-1. Resource Availability as a Function of Subjective Probability

Table 4-1
Alternative Uranium Resource Estimates

Agency or Person	Cost Category	Thousands of Tons of U_3O_8	Remarks
Department of Energy	$\leqslant$ $50/lb	4,170	Includes speculative resource category
Erickson	"currently recoverable"	7,000	
Brink	–	6,000	
EPRI (SR-5)	$\leqslant$ $100/lb	$\geqslant$ 3,500	With a subjective probability of 0.90
		$\geqslant$ 28,900	With a subjective probability of 0.05
A research institute	$\leqslant$ $30/lb	4,000–6,000	(For private client)
Drew	$35/lb	1,900–2,300	25 percent of average profit devoted for exploratory expenditures; $35 is the price per lb of uranium.

Source: M.F. Searl and J. Platt, "Views on Uranium and Thorium Resources," *Annals of Nuclear Industry* 2(1975):760; Energy Research and Development Administration, *Statistical Data of the Uranium Industry,* Grand Junction Office Report GJO-100, Grand Junction, Colorado, p. 43; M.W. Drew, "U.S. Uranium Deposits: A geostatistical Model," *Resources Policy* 13 (March 1977), p. 69. Reprinted by permission of Pergamon Press.

ity of uranium, are shown along with the estimates of others in table 4-1. Included in table 4-1 is the recent study prepared by Drew, who has developed an interesting geostatistical model of the uranium deposits.[4] The estimates of maximum reserves are derived as a function of uranium prices at varying levels of exploration expenditures. The exploration expenditures are expressed as a percentage of the operating profit or in terms of expenditures per pound of uranium discovered (figure 4-2). Increasing proportions of exploratory expenditures provide a greater stimulus for resource discovery, and the potential discoverable reserves of uranium increase as the uranium prices continue to increase. On the assumption that 25 percent of the average profit is devoted to exploration expenditures, approximately 7 million tons of uranium can be supplied at a price of $60 per pound of U_3O_8. The estimates shown here are higher than the ERDA estimates. As a result, these findings enhance the confidence in the ERDA statistics for uranium reserves and resources.

However, a few studies provide conservative estimates and emphasize the resource scarcity and possible adverse impact on the development of nuclear programs. To support the thesis of a limited resource base, the work of Lieber-

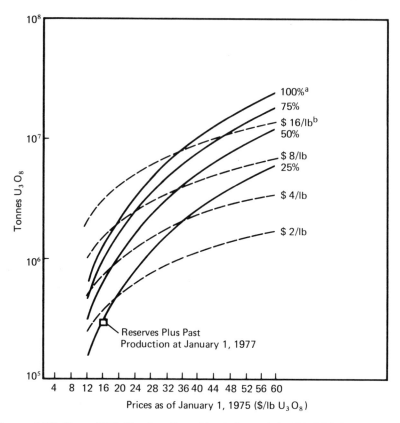

Source: M.W. Drew, "U.S. Uranium Depositis: A Geostatistical Model," *Resources Policy* 12(1977): 69. Reprinted by permission of Science and Technology Press, Ltd.
[a]Percentages indicate the proportion of average profit devoted to exploration.
[b]Dollar values indicate actual exploration expenditures per pound of U_3O_8 discovered.

Figure 4-2. Potential Discoverable Reserves of Uranium in the United States

man has frequently been referred to.[5] This work utilizes the Hubbert type of depletion approach in the estimation of U.S. uranium reserves and resources.

Hubbert Depletion Curves

A commonly used technique for estimating resource availability is the Hubbert depletion curve. According to this method, the cumulative discoveries Q_d are defined as the sum of cumulative production Q_p and proved reserves Q_R. The expected trends in the production, discovery, and reserves of a resource

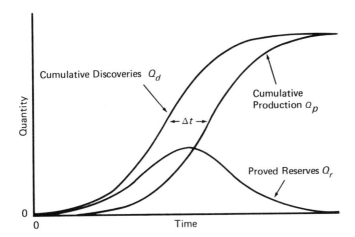

Source: M.K. Hubbert, "Energy Resources," *Resources and Man*, W.H. Freeman and Co., San Francisco, 1969, p. 172. Reproduced from *Resources and Man* with the permission of the National Academy of Sciences, Washington, D.C.

Note: Δt indicates the time lapse between discovery and production.

Figure 4-3. Generalized Form of Curves of Cumulative Discoveries, Cumulative Production, and Proved Preserves for a Petroleum Component During a Full Cycle of Production.

for its life cycle are shown in figure 4-3. The cumulative production begins at zero and increases at an exponential rate as long as the production rate is positive; as the production declines, the cumulative production approaches Q_∞, the ultimate recoverable resource. The cumulative discovery curve follows the same trend as the cumulative production curve, except that it precedes by some time interval Δt. As the cumulative production and cumulative discoveries reach the value Q_∞, the proved reserves will have declined to zero, thereby completing the life cycle of the resource (figure 4-3). This method of analysis has been somewhat successful in the assessment of domestic reserves of oil and gas.[6] This approach has also been used in the study of alternate energy resource availability to the year 2000.[7]

The functional relationship between cumulative production and the ultimate recoverable resource is defined as

$$Q_p = \left(\frac{Ke^{at}}{1 + Ke^{at}} \right)^b Q_\infty$$

The cumulative production ratè is then derived as follows.

$$\ln Q_p = b\{\ln(Ke^{at}) - \ln(1 + Ke^{at})\} + \ln Q_\infty$$

$$\frac{1}{Q_p} \cdot \frac{dQ_p}{dt} = b\left\{a - \frac{Kae^{at}}{1 + Ke^{at}}\right\} = \frac{ab}{1 + Ke^{at}}$$

and

$$\left(\frac{Q_p}{Q_\infty}\right)^{1/b} = 1 - \frac{1}{1 + Ke^{at}}$$

$$\frac{1}{1 + Ke^{at}} = 1 - \left(\frac{Q_p}{Q_\infty}\right)^{1/b}$$

$$\frac{dQ_p}{dt} = abQ_p \frac{1}{1 + Ke^{at}}$$

which is equivalent to

$$abQ_p\left\{1 - \left(\frac{Q_p}{Q_\infty}\right)^{1/b}\right\}$$

Using the Hubbert approach, Lieberman analyzed the statistical data of the uranium-mining industry for the purpose of estimating the ultimate recoverable uranium resource. He establishes the statistical relationship between the uranium discovery rate and the cumulative exploratory footage drilled. By defining the rate of discovery as

$$R(h) = R_0 e^{-\beta h}$$

where R is the rate of discovery and h is the cumulative footage drilled, Lieberman gives the quantity of uranium discovered as a function of cumulative footage drilled.

$$Q_0 = \int_0^{h_0} R(h)dh$$

$$= R_0 \int_0^h \frac{d[-e^{-\beta h}]}{\beta}$$

$$= R_0 \beta^{-1}(1 - e^{-\beta h_0})$$

By letting h_0 take an infinite value, Lieberman calculated the ultimate recoverable resource Q_∞ as follows.

$$Q_\infty = R_0 \beta^{-1}$$

This study found that the total uranium resource availability at $30 or less per pound of U_3O_8 was 1.2 million tons. There were two main criticisms of Lieberman's analysis of ultimate recoverable resource of uranium. One was the statistical methodology that he used in the estimation of uranium resources. The other criticism concerned the size of the estimated resources. Lieberman points out that there are only 1.2 million tons of ultimate recoverable uranium resources. According to ERDA estimates this amount of uranium has already been identified as "reserves," "probable potential," and "cumulative production." A critical review of Lieberman's work was further made by Searl and Platt.[8]

Discrete-Time Logistic Formulation

A new approach has been formulated to test the reliability of the reserve base as estimated by the Department of Energy in a form of a discrete-time problem. The logistic curve equation is

$$Q(t) = \frac{K}{1 + ae^{-rt}}$$

With logarthmic transformation this expression becomes

$$\ln Q(t) = \ln K - \ln (1 + ae^{-rt})$$

The least-square formulation is then given by

$$\min_{K,r,a} f(K,r) = \min_{K,r,a} \sum_j [\ln Q(j) - \ln K + \ln (1 + ae^{-rj})]^2$$

Then taking partial derivatives of K, r, and a gives

$$\frac{\partial f}{\partial K} = \frac{2}{K} \sum_j [\ln Q(j) - \ln K + \ln (1 + ae^{-rj})] = 0$$

$$n \ln \hat{K} = \sum_j \ln Q(j) - \sum_j \ln (1 + ae^{-rj})$$

Similarly

$$\frac{\partial f}{\partial r} = 2 \sum_j [\ln Q(j) - \ln K + \ln (1 + ae^{-rj})] \frac{-aje^{-rj}}{1 + ae^{-rj}} = 0$$

$$\frac{\partial f}{\partial a} = 2 \sum_j [\ln Q(j) - \ln K + \ln (1 + ae^{-rj})] \frac{e^{-rj}}{1 + ae^{-rj}} = 0$$

This formulation, requiring the solution of K, which is treated here as the proved reserves Q_R, is defined mainly in terms of a continuous logistic function.

A discrete formulation of this problem of the continuous logistic curve can be expressed in the form of a difference equation

$$Q_{m+1} - Q_m = rQ_m (1 - Q_m/K)$$

and with Θ_{m+1} set equal to $(Q_{m+1} - Q_m)/Q_m$, the equation then becomes $\Theta_{m+1} = r - rQ_m/K$, where Q_m denotes the cumulative production and reserves. The parameters of the estimated equation for \$10 reserves are $r = 0.5721$ and $r/K = -0.1365 \times 10^{-5}$, which give an estimate for the reserves and cumulative production of the order of 4.190×10^5 tons of uranium for the year 1975. The Department of Energy estimates are 4.824×10^5 tons of uranium, which are close to the present estimates.[9] The estimates for reserves at \$15 per pound of U_3O_8 show similar results. The estimated parameters for this equation were $r = 0.4983$ and $r/K = -0.81767 \times 10^{-6}$, providing a total reserve estimate of 6.09×10^5 tons of U_3O_8.

Nonconventional Sources

One of the early studies of nonconventional sources of uranium was done by Nininger.[10] This study gives information on the amount of uranium available from different sources, the cost of production, and the uranium concentration. Battelle has done a more detailed and comprehensive study on these non-conventional sources.[11] Their work goes into greater depth on the economics as well as the environmental implications of uranium extraction. The Liquid Metal Fast Breeder Reactor Program Review Group discusses the availability of uranium from nonconventional as well as conventional sources in the United States and various other countries.[12]

The main sources of uranium as a direct product and as a by-product from the nonconventional sources are derived from the following resource categories:

Wet process phosphoric acid

Copper leach operations

Uraniferous coal and lignite
    Coal-fired power plant ash
    Lignite gasification plant residue
    Lignite-fired power plant ash

Uranium in extrusive rock

Chattanooga shale

Uranium in seawater

The uranium availability from these sources can be evaluated according to production cost, average grade, recovery rate, resource availability, technology status, and various other social and environmental aspects of these resources. Table 4-2 shows that 1 million to 5 million tons of uranium can be recovered as a by-product from phosphoric acid produced from phosphate rock in the United States and North Africa. The uranium recovered from wet phosphoric acid from Florida phosphate rock was estimated to be around 85 thousand tons and can be recovered at a cost of $10 per pound.[13] Currently the production cost can be as high as $20 per pound of U_3O_8. The average grade of U_3O_8 from this process is estimated to be in the range of 60 ppm to 200 ppm. However, the uranium availability from this category is limited by the production and demand for phosphatic fertilizers.

Similarly the recovery of uranium from copper leach operations provide another low-cost source of uranium with present technology. However, the concentration of uranium from the copper leach operations is much less than that from the wet phosphoric acid processes. The average concentration of U_3O_8 from copper leach operations is estimated to be 1 ppm to 12 ppm. The recovery of uranium is considered feasible, but there is no current estimate for the production of uranium from this source. The total resource availability from this source during the period 1975 to 2000 is said to be in the range of 20 thousand to 35 thousand tons of U_3O_8.

Another important resource category for the supply of uranium is the uraniferous coal and lignite sources. The cost of uranium production varies with the grade of uranium from the coal and lignite residues in the form of ash. Similarly there is a great deal of variation in the concentration of uranium from the coal and lignite sources. The uranium concentration in these sources is estimated to be in the range of 10 ppm to 3000 ppm. At present it is feasible to recover uranium from the ashes of the lignite-fired power plants, and such a recovery appears impossible from the gasification residue because the technology is still not proven in this field.

The uranium concentration in Chattanooga shale varies anywhere from 25 ppm to 50 ppm in shales in areas around eastern Tennessee. This category constitutes the largest potential of uranium supply from the earth's crust. Re-

Table 4-2
Conventional and Nonconventional Sources of Uranium in the United States and Foreign Countries

	Average Deposit Grade (ppm U_3O_8)	Deposit Size Range (Tons U_3O_8)	United States	Foreign
Massive veinlike	3,000–25,000	10,000–100,000	—[a]	Rabbit Lake, Canada; Ranger, Australia
Pegmatites	1,000–2,000	Generally small	—[b]	Bancroft, Canada
Vein (2% of U.S. production)	1,000–25,000	1,000–40,000	Minor (Colorado, Washington)	Great Bear Lake, Canada;[c] Shinkolobwe, Zaire;[c] France
Sandstone (98% of U.S. production)	1,000–5,000	1,000–50,000	Important (Colorado Plateau, Wyoming, Texas)	Niger, Gabon, Argentina
Calcrete	1,000–3,000	10,000–50,000	—[d]	Yeelirrie, Australia
Quartz pebble conglomerate	200–1,500	10,000–200,000	—[e]	Elliot Lake, Canada; Witwatersrand, South Africa
Alaskite	300–400	50,000–150,000	—[f]	Rossing, Southwest Africa
Syenite	100–400	10,000–50,000	—[f]	Ilimaussaq, Greenland
Alum shale	300–400	1,000,000	—[g]	Billingon, Sweden
Phosphates[h]	60–200	1–5 million	Florida, Idaho	North Africa
Shales (U.S.)	25–50	5–10 million	Tennessee	
Lignite and coal[l]	10–3000	1 million (?)	Dakotas	

Granites	10–200	0.1–8 million		Brazil
Copper leaching residues[j]	1–12	20,000–30,000	Utah	?
Seawater	0.003	4 billion		South Africa

Source: Energy Research and Development Administration, *Report of the Liquid Metal Fast Breeder Reactor Program Review Group*, ERDA-1, January 1975, p. 18.

Note: A number of other types of uranium occurrences are known but have not been economic to date. Of particular interest are lake beds, tuffs, rhyolites in California, Nevada, Arizona, Colorado, and Utah.

[a] All occurrences are in Precambrian shield environments not found in the United States.

[b] The Grenville province, which contains Canadian pegmatites, extends into United States Pegmatite areas also known in Appalachians and Rocky Mountains.

[c] Mined out.

[d] Unique geologic occurrence; occurrence in United States unlikely.

[e] Small area in Minnesota and Michigan may contain the formation in which Canadian deposits occur; rest of United States unlikely.

[f] A number of uraniferous igneous rocks have been identified in United States in New England, Rocky Mountains, California, and other areas. Prospects fair for occurrence in 100–300 ppm range.

[g] Occurrence of large deposits of such grade is doubtful, but some possibility exists for developing resources with grades better than 60 ppm.

[h] By-product uranium: Recovery from phosphoric acid produced from Florida phosphate rock is estimated to provide a supply of 70,000 (AEC) to 85,000 (USGS) short tons U_3O_8 between 1971 and 2000 at costs near $10 per pound of U_3O_8. These quantities are controlled by demand for phosphate fertilizer. Much larger amounts could be recovered at high costs if phosphate rock were processed for uranium alone, an alternative that is highly unlikely because of cost.

[i] By-product uranium: In most coals and lignites, uranium concentrations are very low. At an average of 10 ppm U_3O_8, the 700 billion tons of Dakota lignites would contain 7 million tons U_3O_8, but the production rates would be set by the rate at which synthetic gas would be produced. Assuming that 20% of the projected demand for natural gas of the United States in the year 2000 is made from lignite, perhaps 2000 to 3000 short tons of U_3O_8 per year could be produced at approximately 50% yield (no production now planned).

[j] By-product uranium: Uranium concentrations in porphyry copper ores are very low (less than 10 ppm), but recovery of small quantities from acid leach solution has been economically feasible. Between 1975 and 2000, between 20,000 and 35,000 short tons of U_3O_8 might be produced.

source availability estimates range from 5 million to 10 million tons which can be produced at a cost much higher than that from the conventional sandstone deposits.

Another major potential uranium resource is the granites, which are estimated to contain as much as 8 million tons of uranium. The production cost of uranium from this source can be expected to be relatively high in comparison with all other resource categories.

Seawater has frequently been considered a potential source for enormous supplies of uranium. At the present level of technology a potential of 4 billion tons of uranium has been identified for recovery at a production cost of $30 to $1000 per pound of U_3O_8.[14]

Review of the conventional and nonconventional sources of uranium indicates that the United States has sufficient resource base to meet the fuel needs of the maximum nuclear capacity projected by the Department of Energy to the year 2000.

Notes

1. D.P. Harris, *Quantitative Methods for the Appraisal of Mineral Resources,* prepared for the U.S. Energv and Research Development Administration, GJO–6344, January 1, 1977.

2. M.F. Searl and J. Platt, "Views on Uranium and Thorium Resources," *Annals of Nuclear Energy* 2 (1975):751-762.

3. Ibid., p. 759.

4. M.W. Drew, "U.S. Uranium Deposits: A Geostatistical Model," *Resources Policy* 13 (1977):60-69.

5. M.A. Lieberman, "United States Uranium Resources: An Analysis of Historical Data," *Science* 192 (1976):431–436. Another conservative study considers that besides the actual extent of U.S. uranium resources, the productive capability of the uranium industry will be a crucial factor in determining the future availability of uranium in the United States; H.C.McIntyre, *Uranium, Nuclear Power, and Canada–U.S. Energy Relations,* Canadian-American Committee, C.D. Howe Research Institute, Canada, 1978, pp. 22-30.

6. M.K. Hubbert, "Energy Resources," *Resources and Man,* W.H. Freeman and Company, San Francisco, 1969.

7. C.E. Whittle et al., *The IEA Energy Simulation Model,* Oak Ridge Associated Universities, January 1976.

8. M.F. Searl and J. Platt, Letter to the Editor, *Science* 196 (1977): 603-604.

9. Energy Research and Development Administration, *Statistical Data of the Uranium Industry,* Grand Junction Office, Report GJO–100, Grand Junction, Colorado, January 1, 1977, p. 24.

10. R.D. Nininger, "Uranium Reserves and Requirements," in *Nuclear Fuel Resources and Requirements,* WASH-1243, U.S. Atomic Energy Commission, April 1973, pp. 10-27.

11. *Assessment of Uranium and Thorium Resources in the United States and the Effect of Policy Alternatives,* Battelle-Pacific Northwest Laboratories, December 1974.

12. Energy Research and Development Administration, *Report of the Liquid Metal Fast Breeder Reactor Program Review Group,* ERDA-1, January 1975.

13. Ibid., p. 18.

14. Ibid., p. 18.

5 World Uranium Resources

Since the supply of oil in the world has been greatly affected by political and economic factors, many countries are turning to nuclear as their major source of electric power. The question has been raised concerning the adequacy of the world uranium resources. Are the uranium resources sufficient to provide the needed world energy for the next twenty-five years? The sufficiency of world uranium resources will be affected not only by the availability of the physical resource, but also by policies affecting exports of uranium from one country to another. These policies will have a great bearing on the decisions made by the nuclear industry in any country.

Several European countries have well-established nuclear power programs. France, the Soviet Union, and several other countries are well ahead of the United States in their programs on nuclear breeder technology.[1] The future of nuclear programs is important to countries that do not have indigenous energy sources and must depend heavily on the oil imports from the Middle Eastern countries. In many Asian countries nuclear programs have become an integral part of the total energy systems. The future of the world nuclear industry depends on environmental and safety problems, the availability of uranium resources, and the cost of providing the fuel to nuclear reactors. This chapter examines the total resource availability, adequacy of these resources, geographic distribution, and the implications for the growth of the world nuclear industry.

World Uranium Reserves and Resources

The Organization for Economic Cooperation and Development (OECD) study prepared by the Nuclear Energy Agency and the International Atomic Energy Agency provides thus far the most detailed and most valuable information on world uranium resources, production, and demand. The uranium reserves and resources reported by different countries provide the basis for reporting much of the information in this study. The resource category defined here as "reasonably assured" is equivalent to "reserves" used in the analysis of the U.S. uranium-mining industry. Similarly the term "estimated additional resource" corresponds to the "potential resource" category, which includes the "probable" but does not include the "possible" and "speculative" resource categories in U.S. reserve statistics. The reserves and resources are shown for the cost categories of $30 per pound of U_3O_8. As of January 1977 the reserves at a cost less than $30 per pound were estimated to be around 1.65 million tons (table 5-1). The reserve estimates of 1977 showed an increase of 570 thousand tons of uranium over the previous 1975 OECD estimates. An additional 540 thousand tons of uranium are identified in the cost category of $30 to $50 per pound of U_3O_8. The potential resource that can be recovered at a cost of $50 or less per pound of U_3O_8 is estimated to be 2.1 million tons.[2]

There will be a continual upward revision of the world uranium reserves and resources as further exploratory drilling is undertaken in the presence of a stable world nuclear industry. Currently exploration programs are reported in progress in more than fifty countries. The relative share of the Asian and African countries in the world uranium market will also increase as these countries explore new territories for uranium as a source of nuclear fuel and as a possible source of mineral wealth holdings.

Geographical Distribution

The largest known uranium reserve lies in the North American continent. These reserves account for the largest share of the world's total reserves at a cost of $30 per pound of U_3O_8. After the United States, Canada has the largest known uranium reserves and resources in the world. Canada's uranium exploration, development, and export policies are important to the United States because of their geographical proximity as well as the concern for national security.

Canadian production reached a level of 4,850 tonnes with five mines operating in 1976. As early as January 1974 the Canadian government planned to restrict uranium exports to assure the availability of uranium reserves for meeting domestic fuel requirements. It was further advocated that uranium be exported in the most advanced form. Ontario, which possesses 84 percent of the Canadian reserves, asked for the liberalization of federal control over the foreign ownership of the country's uranium industry. One of the motives of the Canadian legislation was to provide fuel requirements for the country for the next thirty years. The Canadian policy with regard to uranium exports is stated as follows.

> To insure sufficient uranium for at least thirty years' reserve for nuclear fuel for all the nuclear power plants in Canada in operation, under construction or planned in the next ten-year period.
>
> To export uranium in the most advanced form, the uranium to be exported with the stipulation that it not be reexported for sale.
>
> To limit the export contracts to a maximum period of ten years.

Table 5-1

Reasonably Assured and Estimated Additional Uranium Resources in Different Countries

(thousands of metric tons of U_3O_8)

Country	Reserves		Resources	
	Less than $30 per Pound of U_3O_8	*$30–$50 per Pound of U_3O_8*	*Less than $30 per Pound of U_3O_8*	*$30–$50 per Pound of U_3O_8*
Algeria	28	0	50	0
Argentina	17.8	24	0	0
Australia	289	7	44	5
Austria	1.8	0	0	0
Bolivia	0	0	0	0.5
Brazil	18.2	0	8.2	0
Canada[a]	167	15	392	264
Central Afrian Empire	8	0	8	0
Chile	0	0	5.1	0
Denmark	0	5.8	0	8.7
Finland	1.3	1.9	0	0
France	37	14.8	24.1	20.0
Gabon	20	0	5	5
Germany, F. R.	1.5	0.5	3	0.8
India	29.8	0	23.7	0
Italy	1.2	0	1	0
Japan	7.7	0	0	0
Korea	0	3	0	0
Madagascar	0	0	0	2.0
Mexico	4.7	0	2.4	0
Niger	160	0	53	0
Philippines	0.3	0	0	0
Portugal	6.8	1.5	0.9	0
Somalia	0	6.2	0	3.4
South Africa	306	42	34	38
Spain	6.8	0	8.5	0
Sweden	1	300	3	0
Turkey	4.1	0	0	0
United Kingdom	0	0	0	7.4
United States[b]	523	120	838	215
Yugoslavia	4.5	2	5	15.5
Zaire	1.8	0	1.7	0
Total (rounded)	1,650.0	540.0	1,510.0	590.0

Source: Organization for Economic Cooperation and Development, *Uranium: Resources, Production, and Demand*, Paris, December 1977, pp. 20–21. Reprinted with permission.

[a]Categories are by reference to prices.

[b]The estimates of reserves and resources shown here for the United States will not agree with the estimates shown in chapter 4 because of the differences in the definition of resources.

To establish a government stockpile of uranium to supplement the fuel supplies.

To insure adequate production capacity for achieving the full potential for domestic nuclear programs.[3]

Recently the Canadian government required 10 percent of the production to be reserved for domestic use and that this proportion be increased to 16 percent by the year 1984. Another matter of concern to Canada with regard to uranium export policy has been nuclear safeguards and the possibility of diversion in nuclear weapons. The government requires that all countries receiving nuclear shipments from Canada must satisfy the proper safeguards of uranium as a fuel for nuclear materials. Countries that fail to adhere to these regulations are deprived of the nuclear supplies from Canada.

The Australian government, like the United States, encouraged uranium exploration and discovery in the early period of development through economic incentives and rewards. The first period lasted from 1947 to 1961, during which several large uranium deposits were discovered. The second period, 1966-1977, marked the participation of large companies using sophisticated technological methods in the discovery of uranium. The present official policy of Australia encourages the private entry and foreign investment in uranium exploration.[4]

The total estimated reserves at a cost of $50 per pound are around 296 thousand tons of uranium. Most of the low-cost Australian uranium reserves are found in the Alligator Rivers Uranium Province containing the Jabiluka, Ranger, Koongarra, and Naberlek deposits of uranium.[5] Currently there is one plant in operation at Mary Kathleen in Queensland, with a nominal annual production capacity of 500 tons of uranium. The Australian government has 42 percent interest in this operation. Recently the government announced its programs to expand and develop the uranium industry at Ranger and to extend its operations in the Northern Territory.

The Australian government has formulated certain policies governing the exploration and production of uranium. The government allows exploration for uranium by domestic as well as by foreign private companies. In matters relating to foreign collaboration the government requires that any exploration project must show an Australian ownership of 75 percent. The Australian uranium export policy has been influenced by political and social issues. The most recent policy emphasis is on the proliferation of nuclear weapons and on the management of radioactive waste material.

The other major uranium deposits are found in South Africa and in South-West Africa. These deposits account for 350 thousand tons of uranium reserves at a cost of $50 per pound. A great deal of interest has been shown in the recovery of uranium as a by-product of gold mining in South Africa.[6] The South African government encourages uranium exploration by local and foreign countries. The estimated production capacity of uranium located at gold mines in 1976 was 2,644 tons of uranium. In South Africa the reserves are located in the gold-bearing quartz pebble conglomerates of the Rand and Orange Free State. The uranium reserves in South-West Africa are in the Rossing Mine. This large reserve is a low-grade alaskite deposit. In Europe, Sweden possesses large deposits of low-grade uranium in the formation of bituminous shale.

Several other countries have undertaken activities relating to uranium exploration and production. These countries are France, Japan, Spain, West Germany, Italy, Indonesia, and the Soviet Union.

Japan has agreed with various other countries concerning the supply of uranium. Japan and France have agreed on production possibilities from the Akouta deposits in the Republic of Niger. Similarly the Japanese consortium, consisting of nine regional electric utilities and a U.S. uranium-producing company, Kerr-McGee, has participated in exploration projects in North and West Africa, Canada, Australia, and South America. The total expenditure incurred on exploration activity in other countries by the Japanese national authority and private companies amounted to approximately $47 million during the period 1972 to 1977.

In France the major exploration and production programs are carried out by the government, much as is done by the governments of Canada and the United States. The major policy of the French government is to be able to meet all domestic uranium needs and to capture 20 percent of the world market.

In Latin America exploration and production have been restricted mainly to the governments. The interest and importance of other countries have not been significant in the exploration and production of uranium.

The 1974 announcement of the Atomic Energy Commission opened the way for foreign imports of uranium. Beyond 1983 the United States must either expand its present production capability to the extent that it can satisfy all domestic needs from internal production or import substantial amounts of foreign uranium. The amount of foreign uranium that will be imported into the United States depends on the world's uranium requirements, production capability, and the world price of uranium.

This discussion of the uranium reserves and resources indicates the presence of an abundance of uranium in different parts of the world. The world's present known reserves and production capacity will be able to support the world nuclear programs for the next twenty years. The adequacy of uranium supplies in providing the uranium requirements of the electric utilities beyond the next two decades depends on the rate at which the capacity of uranium production is increased. The political and economic factors governing the resource development, production, and export of uranium will also affect the level of resource adequacy in meeting the future needs of the nuclear electric industry. Sentiments concerning the proliferation of nuclear weapons are stronger among the nations that have large reserves of uranium. These sentiments affect their policies on the development and export of uranium. The problem of world uranium reserve adequacy in relation to world nuclear capacity forecasts and cumulative uranium requirements is further examined in the following section.

World Nuclear Growth

In the last few years there has been a continuous downward revision of world nuclear capacity forecasts for the year 2000. The declining trend in the world nuclear capacity forecast is evident from the estimates prepared by different agencies over a period of time. In 1975 the OECD estimates for the world nuclear capacity for the year 2000 were in the range of 2,000 GW_e-2,500 GW_e.[7] These estimates were revised to a low of 1400 GW-1650 GW in 1976.[8] Current estimates prepared by OECD for the world nuclear capacity for the year 2000 are in the range of 1000 GW-1890 GW.[9]

The frequent revision in U.S. nuclear forecasts has been one of the reasons for a declining trend in the growth rate of the world installed nuclear generating capacity. Another factor in the lower projections of future world nuclear capacity is the widespread resistance in some of the nuclear countries concerning the environmental and safety aspects of nuclear power programs. U.S. nuclear capacity currently accounts for more than half the total world nuclear generating capacity. The other half of world capacity is shared by Europe and all the other countries, including Japan.[10]

Several countries have embarked on nuclear programs. The estimated nuclear growth in different countries for the period 1975-1990 is shown in table 5-2. From 1980 onward, the nuclear plants become more visible in countries other than the United States. By 1985 nuclear capacity is estimated to be greater than 10 GW in Canada, Germany, France, Japan, Spain, and the United Kingdom. There has been a dramatic change in the forecasts of nuclear power, especially in the last two years. The nuclear power growth estimates provided for different countries in 1975 have been reduced by almost half. Energy conservation measures, effects of worldwide economic recession, are said to be contributing factors in the decline of world nuclear capacity. The downward trend was further accelerated by the uncertainty pertaining to the capability of the nuclear fuel cycle to provide the fuel needs of planned nuclear capacity, solution concerning the disposal of radioactive waste, and public resistance to nuclear power. The world's nuclear capacity is estimated to be in the range of 1,000 GW-1,890 GW in the year 2000. The 1977 estimates of the accelerated case for nuclear capacity in 2000 are less than the low estimates of nuclear made in 1975. The reduction in nuclear capacity is witnessed in all the countries that have embarked on nuclear as a future source of energy. The cumulative

Table 5-2
World Nuclear Power Growth Estimate 1975-1990
(GW$_e$)

Country	1975	1980	1985	1990
Australia	—	0.7	0.7	2
Austria	—	—	—	—
Belgium	1.7	1.7	3.5	8.0
Canada	2.5	6.0	10.0	20.0
Denmark	—	—	—	2.0
Finland	—	2.2	2.2	3.5
France	2.3	15.0	34.0	53.0
Germany	3.2	12.0	25.0	47.0
Greece	—	—	—	1.0
Ireland	—	—	—	—
Italy	0.6	1.4	5.4	25.0
Japan	6.6	15.0	27.0	50.0
Luxembourg	—	—	—	1.0
Netherlands	0.5	0.5	0.5	3.0
New Zeland	—	—	—	—
Norway	—	—	—	—
Portugal	—	—	—	1.8
Spain	1.1	8.0	15.0	20.0
Sweden	3.2	6.5	7.4	8.0
Switzerland	1.0	1.9	2.8	3.0
Turkey	—	—	—	1.0
United Kingdom	4.8	10.3	10.3	15.3
United States	40.1	60.0	115.0	194.0
OECD[a]				
Present Trend Estimate		141.0	259.0	459.0
Accelerated Nuclear Estimate		141.0	343.0	640.0
Non-OECD Countries[b]				
Present Trend		5.0	19.0	45.0
Accelerated		5.0	25.0	60.0
Total				
Present Trend		146.0	278.0	504.0
Accelerated		146.0	368.0	700.0

Source: Organization for Economic Cooperation and Development, *Uranium: Resources, Production, and Demand,* Paris, December 1977, p. 28. Reprinted with permission.

[a]The "present trend" estimates assume the continuation of current patterns of energy consumption and as well the regulatory constraints affecting the construction of nuclear plants. The "accelerated case" assumes the future economic and political environment as being favorable for rapid growth of nuclear power. Some of the factors are assumed to be a continuing fear of oil embargo and lack of availability of fossil fuels.

[b]Countries included here are Algeria, Argentina, Bangladesh, Brazil, Chile, Colombia, Cuba, Egypt, Hong Kong, India, Indonesia, Iran, Iraq, Israel, Korea, Kuwait, Malaysia, Mexico, Niger, Pakistan, Peru, Phillippines, Saudi Arabia, Singapore. Taiwan, Thailand, Union of South Africa, Uruguay, Venezuela.

uranium requirements of the nuclear economy depend on the enrichment tails assay, recycling of uranium and plutonium, reactor mix, and several other technical factors that affect the quantity of uranium required.

Under the assumption that lightwater reactor capacity predominates, figure 5-1 shows the cumulative uranium requirements for the year 2000 as estimated by OECD for different growth rates and for different policies affecting the recycling of uranium. The world cumulative uranium requirements for the "present trend" case are estimated to be around 2 million tons of ura-

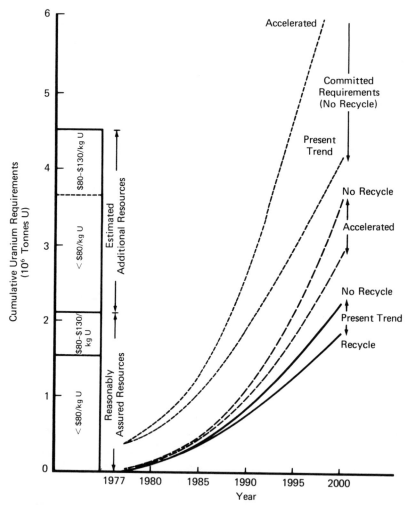

Source: Organization for Economic Cooperation and Development, *Uranium: Resources, Production, and Demand,* Paris, 1977, p. 20. Reprinted with permission.

Figure 5-1. World Cumulative Uranium Requirements, 1977–2000

nium without recycling. These requirements can be met from the world's present known reserves of uranium. The uranium requirements for the "accelerated case," which shows a much faster growth rate than the present trend case, can also be satisfied from the world's present known reserves and resources as shown in Figure 5-1. However, for an accelerated case the lifetime cumulative uranium requirements of the nuclear reactors expected to be in operation in the year 2000 will far exceed the world's present known reserves and resources. The resource problem can be alleviated either by increased worldwide exploratory drilling or by introducing more efficient uranium-conserving nuclear reactors in the world energy economy.

The cumulative uranium requirements are also sensitive to changes in tails assay requirements. An increase of 0.05 percent in the tails assay requirements, for example from 0.25 percent to 0.30 percent, increases uranium requirements by 10 percent. Similarly the requirements decrease by 10 percent if the enrichment tails are decreased from 0.25 percent to 0.20 percent. Another factor that can affect the uranium requirements is the policy concerning the recycling and reprocessing of uranium and plutonium from the nuclear waste. If recycling is allowed, the uranium requirements are expected to decrease by 30 percent of the total requirements.

Notes

1. J.E. Gray et al., *International Cooperation on Breeder Reactors,* Rockefeller Foundation, 1978.

2. Organization for Economic Cooperation and Development, *Uranium: Resources, Production, and Demand,* Paris, 1977, p. 20.

3. Much of the information on foreign uranium supply has come from *Nucleonics Week,* 1974-1977.

4. OECD, *Uranium,* p. 47.

5. Ibid., pp. 47-49; see also Robert J. Wright, "Foreign Uranium Developments," Grand Junction Office, Grand Junction, Colorado, Department of Energy, October 26-27, 1977, pp. 9-12.

6. For a description of geologically favorable areas for the formation of uranium deposits, see OECD, *Uranium,* p. 98.

7. R. Krymm and G. Woite, "Estimates of Future Demand for Uranium and Nuclear Fuel Cycle Services," *International Atomic Energy Agency Bulletin* 18 (1957):7.

8. E.J. Hanrahan, R.H. Williamson, and R.W. Bowen, "World Requirements and Supply of Uranium," paper presented at Atomic Industrial Forum, 1976.

9. OECD, *Uranium,* p. 28.

10. Ibid., p. 79; see also, John A. Patterson, "Foreign Uranium Sources, Status and Development," paper presented at American Nuclear Society, Monterey, California, January, 23-26, 1977, p. 1.

6

Historical Supply Factors

A continuous and reliable supply of fuel is essential for planning in the electric power industry. Supplying uranium is the first as well as the most important step in nuclear fuel cycle operations. In this chapter some of the historical aspects of uranium supply, exploration, and mining and milling operations are discussed.

Historical Uranium Supply

The uranium production series for the period 1947–1977 can be divided into two parts for the purpose of statistical and economic analysis. These two periods are distinguished by the degree of participation by government and private industry in the uranium market. The years from 1947 to 1968 represent the period during which the Atomic Energy Commission (AEC) had great control over the production and price of uranium. Therefore the variations in the uranium supply from 1947 to 1968 cannot be explained in terms of a price-induced market mechanism reflecting the potential supply of uranium resource. During this period the AEC purchased uranium directly from the producers, and the fluctuations in the production level were due mainly to institutional arrangements rather than to economic factors. Figure 6-1 shows the trends in uranium production, drilling, and ore reserves in relation to historical factors.

The period 1968–1970 shows participation by government and by private industry in generating the demand for uranium. Since 1970, private industry has been the only buyer of uranium. The uranium supply, as shown in figure 6-1, is influenced not only by price and government regulations, but also by factors such as major discovery, addition to reserves, and environmental and social factors. This chapter discusses briefly the historical trends affecting the uranium supply and then provides a rational basis for developing an economic framework for projecting the long-term trends in the supply of uranium production.

During the period 1948–1960 the annual production increased from 100 tons to 18,000 tons per year. The increase of production capacity to this level is attributed mainly to the government ore programs, which guaranteed uranium prices and other production bonuses. These measures were taken by the AEC primarily to develop a successful commercial uranium market for the future nuclear power industry and to assure economic markets for successful

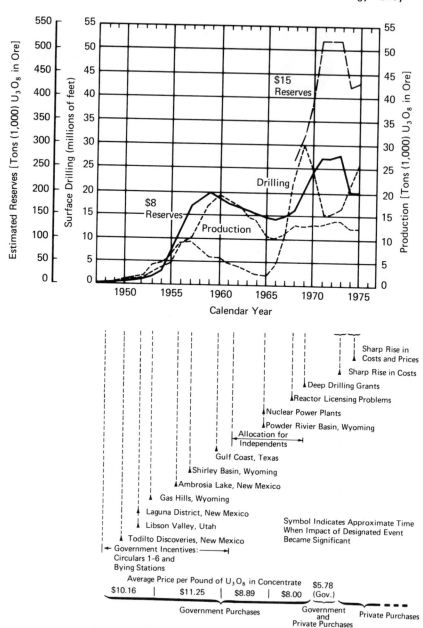

Source: Energy Research and Development Administration, *Statistical Data of the Uranium Industry,* Grand Junction Office Report GJO-100(76), Grand Junction, Colorado, 1976, p. 20.

Figure 6-1. Drilling, Reserves, and Production of Ore Related to Various Historical Factors.

ventures. Prior to 1960 almost all the uranium supplied was to meet the defense needs. After 1960 the supply of uranium was geared to meeting the needs of civilian nuclear power. From 1960 to 1966 the annual production of uranium declined to a level of 10,100 tons. This declining trend was due mainly to curtailment of the government programs. However, the production increased to a level of 13,100 tons in 1970, when the government procurement plans were terminated. During the years 1960 to 1970 both government and private industry participated in generating the demand for uranium. Since 1970, private purchases have been the main force in generating demands for nuclear fuels.

The entry of private industry in the uranium market created a favorable environment for the development and expansion of mining and milling operations. However, the optimism concerning the rapid growth in nuclear power which was likely to create a high demand for uranium did not materialize. The year 1968 witnessed considerable escalations in the capital costs of nuclear plants brought about by the delays in construction and by environmental regulations. The immediate effect of the unexpected developments in the nuclear industry was delays and some cancellations of nuclear plants. As a result, the electric utilities were unwilling to enter into long-term contracts for the supply of uranium, and this action further dampened the uranium price in the private markets. In figure 6-1 the effect is seen in terms of declining drilling activity and uranium production. This declining trend continued through 1971. Finally the level of economic operations reached the bottom in 1972. To reverse the downward trend in the uranium-mining industry, a great deal of effort was directed toward pointing out the urgency for expanding the production facility and other operations to be able to meet the fuel needs of the projected nuclear electric capacity. A dramatic event, the OPEC oil embargo, reversed the downward trend in drilling and production of uranium. The oil embargo gave a big upsurge to the nuclear industry in terms of rapid increases in uranium prices. The indications are that the level of activity will continue on the upswing and that uranium production will continue to increase. The data on uranium production and cumulative production are given in table 6-1. The use of the data in their present form gives rise to a problem in forecasting the long-term trends in the supply of uranium production. The production data for the period 1948-1968 show the effect of government intervention in the market and therefore cannot be pooled with the industry output for the period 1968-1977 without appropriate statistical tests. One can apply, for example, G. Chow's test for determining significant differences in the two production series with and without government intervention in uranium markets.[1] Another way would be to use the production data for the period 1970-1977 which cover only the period of private markets. The latter case will restrict the number of observations for a meaningful statistical analysis. In this study Chow's test has been used for testing the time series wherever the influence of government has been observed.

Another interesting apsect of the historical production is the reserve-to-

Table 6-1

Uranium Production and Cumulative Production, 1947-1976

(tons of U_3O_8)

Year	Production[a]	Cumulative Production
1947	–	–
1948	100	100
1949	500	600
1950	800	1,400
1951	1,100	2,500
1952	1,300	3,800
1953	2,300	6,100
1954	3,500	9,600
1955	4,400	14,000
1956	8,400	22,400
1957	9,800	32,200
1958	14,000	46,200
1959	17,400	63,600
1960	18.800	82,400
1961	18,500	100,900
1962	17,100	118,000
1963	14,700	132,700
1964	13,900	146,600
1965	10,600	157,200
1966	10,100	167,300
1967	10,900	178,200
1968	12,800	191,000
1969	12,600	203,600
1970	13,100	216,700
1971	13,100	229,800
1972	13,900	243,700
1973	13,800	257,500
1974	12,600	270,100
1975	12,300	282,400
1976	14,000	296,400

Source: Energy Research and Development Administration, *Statistical Data of the Uranium Industry,* Grand Junction Office Report GJO-100(77), Grand Junction, Colorado, p. 24.

[a]Includes miscellaneous U_3O_8 receipts from nine waters, heap leach, solution mining, and refining residues.

production series. A reserve-to-production ratio indicates the resource supply in years for a given level of production. A ratio of at least 10 to 1 is generally considered prudent, as there is a considerable lag in the development and supply of a resource. As figure 6-2 shows, oil and gas, the primary domestic energy resources which are becoming scarce, have the lowest ratio of reserves to annual production. The reserve-to-production ratio for the uranium reserves at $10 per pound is well above the ratios for oil and gas and has remained close to 20 for

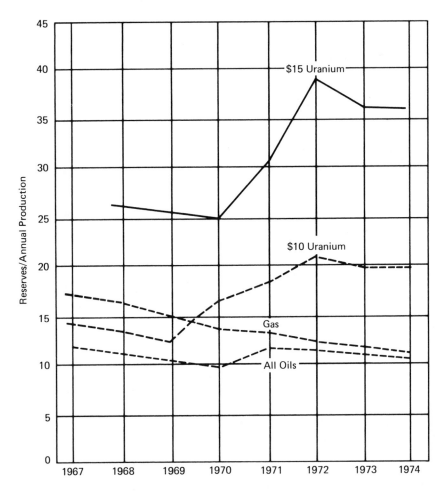

Source: R.T. Zitting, "Estimation of Potential Uranium Resources," *Mineral Resources and the Environment, Reserves, and Resources of Uranium in the United States,* National Academy of Sciences, Washington, D.C., 1975, p. 152.

Figure 6-2. Ratio of Reserves to Production for Oil, Gas, and Uranium.

the last five years. The ratio of reserves to production for higher-cost categories is over 35.

Exploration Activities

Drilling may be for exploration or for development. Exploration for uranium requires huge expenditures and coordination and management of many geophysical and geological studies. Exploration ventures are risky. They involve the selection of a potential area in which reconnaissance on a large scale is undertaken. Airborne surveys may include gamma spectrometry and geophysical techniques, and ground work involves geological, geochemical, and radiometric surveys. Limited drilling can determine the degree of success that can be achieved from this investment. The next step in this process is to acquire the land for drilling. Exploration is now confined primarily to sandstone deposits, which are found in lands owned by the federal government, American Indians, and others. Acquiring land for this purpose has been easy, with the exception of preparing the environmental impact statements for the lands owned by the American Indians. Once the drilling is done, the holes are logged by probes to determine the radioactivity, resistivity, and other geophysical features for evaluation of the drilling results.[2]

There are possibilities of reducing the exploration costs through technological progress. A technique known as track etching seems to reduce the exploration costs by a factor of three to ten. This method uses a special film that is sensitive to the alpha emissions of radon but insensitive to gamma and beta rays. This film is inserted into a cup which is then sunk into the ground; the cup is retrieved after an exposure of more than three weeks, thus providing the necessary data for computer analysis. This procedure helps determine the presence or absence of the uranium ore body and the outline of the field. This technique can cover an area as large as thirty square miles and can detect uranium ore at depths ranging from three hundred to five hundred feet.[3]

Research efforts have recently been directed to the use of helium in the discovery of deeply buried deposits of uranium. The research, supported by the Energy Research and Development Administration (ERDA), the U.S. Geological Survey, and the Electric Power Research Institute (EPRI), will help determine hard-to-find deposits and may considerably reduce the exploratory drilling and expenditures for exploration.[4]

The location and extent of development drilling are determined after exploratory drilling is completed. Development drilling is done around the area close to the selected production centers and can be either surface or underground drilling, depending on the characteristics of the mining deposit. This drilling may continue for periods of two years or more.

Exploration Expenditures

The exploration expenditures determine the level of exploration and development drilling. Drilling activities are significant in the discovery of uranium resources and in uranium production. A statistical summary of U.S. uranium exploration activities is given in table 6-2.

The costs of land holdings and acquisitions shown in table 6-2 include land fees, mineral fees, leases, patented and unpatented claims, and fees for

Table 6-2
U.S. Domestic Exploration Activities, 1966-1978

Year	Land Acquired		Exploration Drilling		Development Drilling		Total Surface Drilling		Other Expenditures	Total Expenditures
	Millions of Acres	Millions of $	Millions of Feet	Millions of $	Millions of Feet	Millions of $	Millions of Feet	Millions of $	Millions of $	Millions of $
1966	1.64	2.24	.93	1.36	1.50	1.24	2.43	2.60	3.55	8.39
1967	4.13	7.57	3.87	6.18	2.92	2.32	6.79	8.50	8.76	24.82
1968	6.50	18.52	12.87	18.53	3.73	2.82	16.60	21.35	13.58	53.45
1969	3.56	13.89	19.69	24.85	4.79	4.34	24.48	29.19	15.67	58.75
1970	2.02	10.74	16.91	21.69	3.41	3.49	20.32	25.18	16.29	52.21
1971	1.49	9.75	11.80	17.00	3.08	4.00	14.88	21.00	10.50	41.25
1972	1.36	4.70	11.95	15.40	3.08	2.70	15.03	18.10	9.60	32.40
1973	2.82	7.67	11.76	19.50	5.25	5.80	17.01	25.27	16.53	49.47
1974	2.32	12.61	14.72	34.90	6.84	9.80	21.56	44.76	21.71	79.08
1975	3.48	16.70	15.69	51.90	9.73	21.90	25.42	73.81	31.52	122.03
1976	4.75	13.89	20.36	70.70	14.44	38.30	34.80	109.00	47.79	170.65
1977	—	—	28.70	—	20.50	—	49.20	—	—	236.20
1978	—	—	30.40	—	17.50	—	47.90	—	—	251.40

Source: Energy Research and Development Administration, *Uranium Exploration Expenditures in 1975 and plans for 1976-1977*, Grand Junction Office, GJO-103(76), Grand Junction, Colorado; W.L. Chenoweth, "Exploration Activities," Grand Junction Office, Grand Junction, Colorado, October 1977.

options to purchase mineral rights. The cost of land acquired for exploration varies anywhere from less than 10¢ to more than $60 per acre, the average cost being $4.80 per acre.[5]

Another important expense is the surface drilling costs. The total surface drilling costs include exploration and development drilling. Exploration drilling accounts for more than 50 percent of the total drilling from 1968 to 1978. The average cost of drilling per foot is estimated at about $2.90 and ranges from a low of $1 to a high of $17 per foot drilled. Exploration costs in the future are expected to increase when the drilling depth is increased and the exploration is extended to areas beyond the known production districts. However, the efforts of private industry in uranium exploration will be greatly facilitated by the National Uranium Resource Evaluation (NURE) exploring activities in reconnaissance and surveys of surface and ground waters. In the model simulation the exploration costs are assumed to remain constant during the period 1977-2000.

Mining and Milling

There are two types of mining for uranium. One method is open-pit mining, where the stripping starts approximately eighteen months prior to ore production and lasts for ten years. The other is underground mining, where shaft sinking starts at the eighth year of the enterprise. By the end of the tenth year the shaft sinking and other preproduction work and mine development will have been completed. The construction of the mill for processing the ore takes approximately two years before the production of uranium can start.

Some of the major unit operations or unit processes included in the activity are ore receiving and crushing, grinding, leaching, liquid-solid separation, purification, precipitation, drying, and packaging. Costs incurred in connection with the mine development, the mine plant and equipment, and the mill construction make up the capital costs of the total costs of the mining and milling activities. These account for approximately 20 percent of the total cost for uranium concentrate production. The ratio of mine and mill capital costs to total costs decreases as the production capacity of the mine increases. Similarly the capital costs increase as the grade of uranium ore extracted decreases, leading to a smaller percentage of uranium recovery. The operating cost also varies with the scale of operations and the grade of ore extracted. A parametric study of the effect of ore grade and production rate on total production costs is shown in figure 6-3. The effect of scale is not pronounced when compared with the effect of decrease in ore grade on total production cost. However, the production cost shown in figure 6-3 does not provide a detailed breakdown of the cost per pound of U_3O_8. Typical capital and operating costs for an underground mining and milling capacity expected to start operation by 1980 are shown in table 6-3. The increase in the production cost from

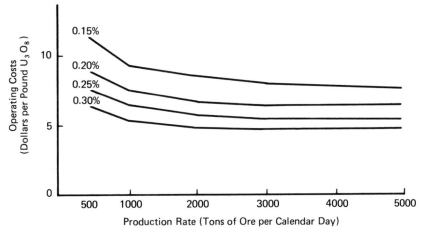

Figure 6-3. Operating Costs as a Function of Production Rate and Ore Grade

Table 6-3

Anticipated Range of Capital Requirements and Production Costs for New Underground Facilities Commencing Operation in 1980

(in 1975 dollars)

Costs	Low[a]	High[b]
Capital investment (millions of dollars)	34	73
Cost breakdown (dollars per pound of U_3O_8)		
Capital		
Acquisition	0.15	0.30
Mine primary development	0.70	1.35
Mine plant and equipment	0.15	0.25
Mill construction	0.40	0.89
Total	1.40	2.70
Operating		
Mining	3.35	7.15
Hauling	0.25	0.45
Milling	1.40	2.90
Royalty	0.50	0.50
Total	5.50	11.00
Total production cost	6.90	13.70

Source: Edison Electric Institute, *Nuclear Fuels Supply,* New York, March 1976, p. 92.

Note: The range between low and high as estimated by the S.M. Stoller Corporation is based on extrapolation of past variations in ore grade, size of production center, mine operating conditions, etc., and making some allowance for the effect of recent price increases.

[a]Assumes capacity of 2,000 tons of ore per calendar day, operation 300 days per year, ten-year life, and ore grade of 0.2 percent.

[b]Assumes capacity of 3,000 tons of ore per calendar day, operation 300 days per year, ten-year life, and ore grade of 0.15 percent.

$6.90 to $13.70 shown in Table 6-3 is said to be mainly due to the decrease in ore grade from 0.20 percent to 0.15 percent.

Many factors affect the increase or decrease in the production cost per pound of uranium. Noteworthy factors are the technology, productivity of factor inputs, scale of operation, environmental regulations, and the average ore grade. Of these factors, the ore grade is considered the most important one affecting the future production cost of uranium. It is difficult to postulate which future developments in environmental legislation will necessitate changes to minimize the adverse effects on the environment. For a detailed analysis of radioactive waste treatment costs and the environmental impact of waste effluents in the nuclear fuel cycle, one should refer to recent works in this area.[6]

The future trends in ore grade depend on the cumulative quantity of uranium produced and the manner in which the reserve and resource are depleted over a period of time. An examination of the future trends in ore grade indicates that as much as a million tons of U_3O_8 can be supplied at $30 or less per pound of U_3O_8 by mining 0.9 percent U_3O_8 ore grade.[7]

Notes

1. J. Kmenta, *Elements of Econometrics,* Macmillan, New York, 1971, pp. 373-374.

2. D.O. Cooper and N.A. Grant, "Economics of Uranium Operations," *Annual Conference of the Atomic Industrial Forum,* San Francisco, California, 1969.

3. *Nucleonics Week* 15 (1974).

4. *Nucleonics Week* 17 (1976).

5. Energy Research and Development Administration, *Uranium Exploration Expenditures in 1975 and Plans for 1976-1977,* Grand Junction Office, Report GJO-103 (1976), Grand Junction, Colorado, p. 2.

6. W.H. Pechin et al., *Correlation of Radioactive Waste Treatment Costs and the Environmental Impact of Waste Effluents in the Nuclear Fuel Cycle for Use in Establishing "as Low as Practicable" Guides; Fabrication of Light-Water Reactor Fuel from Enriched Uranium Dioxide,* ORNL/TM-4902, May 1975; M.B. Sears et al., *Correlation Guides, Milling of Uranium Ores,* ORNL/TM-4903, vols. 1, 2, May 1975; W.S. Groenier et al., *Correlation of Guides; Fabrication of Light-Water Reactor Fuels Containing Plutonium,* ORNL/TM-4904, May 1975; Ledwig W. Koch, "Cost Trends," paper presented at the American Nuclear Society Conference on Uranium Fuel Supply, Monterey, California, January 23-26, 1977.

7. The Grand Junction Office of the Department of Energy has developed programs known as "Could" and "Need" capability programs. The "Need" capability program generates optimal production schedules that minimize the

present worth of industry's total production costs. These programs reinforce the fact that the outputs necessary to meet the fuel needs of projected nuclear capacity by the year 2000 can come from $30 or less per pound U_3O_8 with average ore grade 0.9 percent U_3O_8; see John Klemenic, "Production Capability and Supply," Grand Junction Office, Energy Research and Development Administration, October 1977.

7 Uranium Supply Analysis

The historical aspects of uranium supply provide a rational basis for developing a theoretical framework for the analysis and projections of future trends in the reserves and supply of uranium. Econometric modeling of the supply and demand for minerals has gained considerable interest in recent years. The commodity models are generally developed for forecasting and policy development. The approach used depends on the unique characteristics of the industry modeled. No parallel can be drawn for developing some of the basic characteristics of the uranium mining and milling operations from other established industries. The uranium mining and milling industry is different from other industries in its historical experiences and in its future in view of the uncertainty of future demand, technological developments, and social and institutional factors affecting the industry. Uranium as a fuel is closely related to the oil and gas industries. In the analysis of supply, uranium mining and milling operations seem to have a greater affinity toward the nonferrous metals, such as copper, lead, zinc, and the other precious metals, gold, silver, and platinum.[1] An overview of a few studies of modeling mineral supply is given by developing a supply function for the uranium-mining industry.

Uranium and Other Minerals

A great deal of research in the econometric modeling of metals and minerals has been done at Charles River Associates. Some of the industries examined by this organization were aluminum, copper, lead, zinc, nickel, molybdenum, magnesium, platinum, tungsten, cobalt, and mercury.[2] According to production characteristics the uranium supply is analogous to the supply of nonferrous metals as well as to the supply of petroleum and natural gas. In the dynamic modeling of the supply of tungsten, similar to uranium, Burrows formulated two relationships which account for the different patterns of distributed lags.[3] The relationship that specifies supply as a function of distributed lag of prices was described as

$$q_t^s = \gamma_0 + \gamma_1 \sum_{i=1}^{\infty} \lambda^i P_{t-1}, \qquad 0 \leqslant \lambda < 1$$

and the fomulation that defined the distributed lag on prices to be of inverted form was described as

$$q_t^s = \alpha + \beta_1 \sum_{i=0}^{m} \lambda_i P_{t-1} + \beta_2 Z_t + U$$

where P refers to prices and Z is an exogenous variable. Similarly a well-known world copper industry model specifies the supply relationship as a function of current and past prices.[4] The weighted past prices decline geometrically:

$$q_t^s = \alpha + \mu\beta \sum_{K=0}^{\infty} \lambda^K P_{t-k}, \qquad \lambda = 1 - \mu$$

where $\mu\beta$ represents the short-run effects on supply and the long-run effects by β. In the evaluation of the model for policy development the supply function for the world copper industry was found inadequate and was revised to include the resource availability in explaining the copper supply.[5]

There are models of the gas and the oil industries that explain the structure of the industry and forecast production and prices for alternative economic policies. Well-known gas models have been developed by MacAvoy and Pindyck, Khazzom, and Erickson and Spann.[6] These models explain the production of gas in relation to the level of reserves, production costs, and prices. Similarly there are petroleum industry models that are more akin to the structure and the operations of uranium exploration and mining.[7] The supply models of fuel and nonfuel industries provide some indication in the modeling of producers' behavior in the supply of uranium reserves and production.

Uranium Supply Curves

Two types of supply curves are identified for the uranium mining and milling operations. The short-term supply curve defines the economic relationship between the quantity produced and the uranium price for a fixed level of mining milling capacity. In the past the supply of uranium production has been responsive to changes in uranium prices. For the period during which private purchases generated the demand price for uranium, the shape of the supply curve is shown in figure 7-1. Assume that at price OP_0 the quantity produced is OQ_0. An increase in the price of uranium from OP_0 to OP_1 should cause an increase in output, in the short run, from OQ_0 to OQ_2. However, this trend has not been observed in the production of uranium. The uranium deposits of higher-grade ore may not be

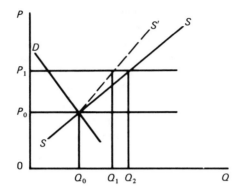

Figure 7–1. Effect of Price Increase on Short-Run Uranium Supply

discovered easily. The producers may turn to low-grade ores for immediate production. The result seems to be an evident increase in the total production of ore but a decrease in the actual supply of U_3O_8 because of lower concentration of uranium from the incremental supplies.[8]

It is the long-run supply curve that is important to this study. In the long run producers can vary production capacity and adapt themselves to changing technologies for improving efficiency in production methods. Under the assumption that firms enter and leave the mining and milling industry in response to the market price, the shifts in the supply curve are postulated in figure 7–2. The curve *SS* is more elastic than the short-run supply curve *ss.* The upward

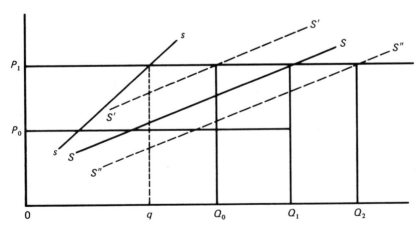

Figure 7–2. Long-Run Uranium Supply Curve

shift in the supply curve $S'S'$ is assumed to result, for example, from future environmental legislation requiring stricter environmental controls and additional costs in the production of uranium, and a downward shift $S''S''$ is possible from factors such as the technological progress in mining and milling of uranium. For a price increase from OP_0 to OP_1 the short-run output $0q$ will gradually increase to a level of $0Q_1$ in the long-run, which will be made possible by the entry of new firms as the economic incentives of price increases become apparent. The degree to which the long-run output will be affected by the various factors is difficult to ascertain at this time.

Modeling the Supply Side

Decisions made by producing firms exhibit a sequential pattern affecting the various stages of the supply of uranium production. The decision to undertake exploratory drilling one year affects the level of development drilling the following year. There is therefore a recursiveness in the facets of the operations of the uranium supply. Each step in the development of reserves and the production of uranium is carefully linked by preserving the economic reasoning supported by statistical inference. Alternative formulations of the model exist, and some of these specifications are discussed.

Equation 7.1 shows the relationship between the amount of exploratory drilling and the variables affecting the level of drilling activity. The following equation is selected for estimation and for inclusion in the model simulation.

$$\log EXD_t = \alpha + \beta_1 \log EXD_{t-1} + \beta_2 \log PU_{t-1} \\ + \beta_3 \log EXPD_t \tag{7.1}$$

where

   EXD = exploratory drilling (million feet)

   PU = price of uranium (dollars per pound of U_3O_8)

   $EXPD$ = exploratory expenditures (millions of dollars)

The "expectations" of future uranium markets play an important role in the decisions made by firms in the exploration of uranium resources. One such factor is the expectation concerning the future demand for uranium, which is reflected in the preceding year's drilling effort. In equation 7.1 this effect is explained by EXD_{t-1}. An upward movement in drilling is supported and reinforced by the past year's drilling statistics. This trend continues until a pessimism creeps into the markets and the drilling activity suddenly takes a downward trend. Such peaks and bottoms in the drilling activity over a period of time are evident in figure 6-1. Future uranium prices also play a significant role in the determination of exploratory drilling. The level of current drilling is generally influenced by the previous year's price of uranium. Finally the level of planned expenditures on the exploratory drilling affects the level of exploration in a given year. Another way of showing the effect of exploration expenditures is to calculate the user costs, which in turn explain the long-run equilibrium level of uranium reserves, as done by Erickson for oil reserves. The user cost has been defined as a measure of the implicit price of the firm embodied in the resource reserves.

$$UC = EXC \frac{r(1 - T\alpha) + \delta(1 - T\alpha - Tv)}{1 - T + T\rho}$$

where

UC = user cost of uranium reserves

EXC = exploration costs

r = cost of capital

T = corporate income tax rate

α = fraction of capital expenditure that can be expended immediately

δ = rate of depreciation of capital stock or reserves

v = fraction of capital expenditure that is depreciable for tax purposes

ρ = rate of percentage depletion

In this uranium study the exploration expenditures affect the drilling activities, which in turn determine the addition to reserves and reserve levels.[9]

The relationship between drilling and expenditures, however, is open to argument when one views drilling as a determining factor rather than a result of the level of expenditures. The exploratory expenditures are treated as an exogenous variable. These expenditures are assumed to be planned by the industry and depend on the financial policies and economic status of the firms participating in uranium exploration. The exploration costs per pound of uranium discovered have not yet been mentioned. It is generally believed that the increasing discovery costs will tend to decrease the level of drilling. On the basis of the review of the exploration costs in chapter 6, exploration costs should remain constant during the next twenty-five years. Some studies have indicated the possibility of a decline in the exploration costs per pound of U_3O_8.[10] Therefore these costs are not included in this formulation of the exploratory drilling.

Perl proposed an alternative formulation of the model for developing a long-term uranium supply curve.[11]

$$DC = e^{\beta_0 + \beta_1 T} D^{\beta_2} \qquad (7.1a)$$

$$TEC = \lambda DC \qquad (7.1b)$$

where

DC = cost of exploratory and developmental drilling

D = exploratory and developmental drilling

T = time

TEC = total expenditures on exploration

This formulation establishes the relationship between the expenditures for exploration and development as a function of the level of drilling. Perl then used the information on costs of exploration and development obtained in equation 7.1a to calculate the total expenditures on exploration.

Since development drilling follows exploratory drilling, the relationship between development drilling and exploratory drilling was established with a lag of one year:

$$\log DD_t = \alpha + \beta \log EXD_{t-1} \qquad (7.2)$$

The exploratory drilling and the development drilling determined in equations 7.1 and 7.2 provide the information on the expected total surface drilling. The identities in this block are

$$TD_t = EXD_t + DD_t \qquad (7.3)$$

$$CDR_t = TD_t + \sum_{k=1}^{t-1} TD_k \qquad (7.4)$$

$$DND_t = TD_t/DPH_t \qquad (7.5)$$

where CDR is cumulative drilling, DND is the total number of holes drilled, and DPH refers to the average depth of the hole drilled. In the model simulations equations 7.3–7.5 were used to provide the necessary information for linking the supply block with the reserve block. The relationship between supply block and resource block is shown in equation 3.4:

$$\log \Delta RR_t = \alpha + \beta_1 \log CDR_{t-1} + \beta_2 \log DND_{t-1}$$

and the estimated quantity of addition to reserves (ΔRR_t) is used in the calculation of the uranium reserve situation:

$$RR_t = RR_{t-1} - q_t^s + \Delta RR_t \tag{7.6}$$

Finally, the uranium reserves enter the estimation of the supply function, along with the price of uranium:

$$\log q_t^s = \alpha + \beta_1 \log RR_{t-1} + \beta_2 \log PU_{t-1} \tag{7.7}$$

In the development of a model for the gas industry MacAvoy and Pindyck have shown that prices directly affect gas production.[12] The uranium price was shown to have a direct affect on the drilling activity (equation 7.1), which determined the level of reserves in a given year. However, the reserve level alone cannot entirely explain the quantity of uranium produced each year. The price of uranium was also considered to affect the decisions made by the uranium producers directly. Equation 7.7a is an alternate for the quantity produced, where the addition to reserve ΔRR replaces the total reserve in explaining the supply of uranium production:

$$\log q_t^s = \alpha + \beta_1 \log \Delta RR_{t-1} + \beta_2 \log PU_{t-1} \tag{7.7a}$$

Equation 7.7a was estimated but not used in the model simulation.

Notes

1. S.S. Merwin, "Uranium: The Exploration Prices and Recent Developments," paper presented at American Nuclear Society Conference on Uranium Supply, Monterey, California, January 23–26, 1977.

2. *Economic Analysis of the Aluminum Industry,* Charles River Associates, 1971; *Economic Analysis of Lead/Zinc Industry.* Charles River Associates, 1967 and 1969; several similar studies were done for magnesium, platinum, cobalt, and mercury by the Charles River Associates.

3. J.C. Burrows, "Econometric Modeling of Metal and Mineral Industries," in *Mineral Materials Modeling,* ed. W.A. Vogley, Johns Hopkins Press,

Baltimore, Md., 1975, pp. 129-132; W.C. Labys, *Dynamic Commodity Models: Specification, Estimation, and Simulation,* D.C. Heath, Lexington, Mass., 1973, pp. 35-58.

4. F.M. Fisher, P.H. Cootner, and M.N. Bailey, "An Econometric Model of the World Copper Industry," *Bell J. Econ.* 3 (1972):568-609.

5. J.W. Carlson, "Mineral Models and Policy Decisions," in *Mineral Materials Modeling,* pp. 21-41.

6. P.W. MacAvoy and R.S. Pindyck, "Alternative Regulatory Policies for Dealing with the Natural Gas Shortages," *Bell J. Econ. Man. Sci.* (1973):454-498; J.D. Khazzoom, "The FPC Staffs' Econometric Model of Natural Gas Supply in the United States," *Bell J. Econ. Man. Sci.* (1971):51-93; E. Erickson and R. Spann, "Supply Response in a Regulated Industry: The Case of Natural Gas," *Bell J. Econ. Man. Sci.* 2 (1971):94-121.

7. P. Rice, "An Econometric Model of the U.S. Petroleum Industry," Ph.D. Thesis, State University of New York, Stony Brook, 1976.

8. Electric Power Research Institute, *Uranium Price Formation,* EA-498-1977, pp. 10-27.

9. E. Erickson et al., "Oil Supply and Tax Incentives," *Brookings Paper on Economic Activity,* Brookings Institution, Washington, D.C., 1974; R.E. Hall and D.W. Jorgenson, "Tax Policy and Investment Behavior," *American Economic Review* 57 (1967):391-414.

10. Edison Electric Institute, *Nuclear Fuels Supply,* New York, March 1976, pp. 89-90.

11. Lewis J. Pearl, "The GESMO Utility Group on U_3O_8 Prices," Testimony before the GESMO Hearing Board, U.S. Nuclear Regulatory Commission, April 14, 1977, p. 18.

12. P.W. MacAvoy and R.S. Pindyck, "Regulatory Policies for Dealing with the Gas Shortages," *Bell J. Econ. Man. Sci.* 4 (1973):454-498; R.S. Pindyck, "The Regulatory Implications of Three Alternative Econometric Supply Models of Natural Gas," *Bell J. Econ. Man. Sci.* 5 (1974):633-645.

8 Uranium Imports, Exports, and Inventory

The total uranium availability in a given year can be expressed in the following relationship.

$$Q_t^s = q_t^s + (IMP_t - EXP_t) - INV_t$$

where *IMP* denotes imports, *EXP* denotes exports, and *INV* represent the inventory held by different agencies. The inclusion of imports and exports in the calculation of total uranium availability indicates that uranium is actively traded in the world uranium market. Currently the volume of uranium in international trade is negligent for any serious analysis or consideration for its impact on any economy. This trend may change, thus affecting the domestic uranium industry. The imports of uranium in large quantities will attract the attention of many analysts and policymakers, as the oil embargo has had a serious impact on the U.S. economy. At the present uranium imports do not present any serious problem and are therefore not included in the model simulation. However, the present trends in the imports and exports of uranium and the future implications of these developments are identified.

U.S. Imports

Uranium imports may become a necessity for several reasons. If a country has no uranium deposits and embarks on nuclear programs, then supplies must come from other countries. This is true in the case of Japan and West Germany, since they must rely on outside imports of uranium. Another such situation would be one in which the domestic needs of uranium exceed the domestic supply and the remainder must be filled from outside sources. Such a case is likely for the United States if the domestic production capacity does not keep pace with requirements for uranium. In a competitive environment the imports will increase whenever the foreign price for uranium is cheaper than the domestic price. All these factors will have some effect on the future production-to-import ratio for the United States.

In October 1974 it was announced that the import restrictions on uranium of foreign origin will be lifted on a gradual basis beginning in 1977, when 10 percent of the feed furnished to domestic utilities can be foreign uranium. This percentage of feed due to imports will be increased each year so that the restrictions will be taken off completely in 1984.[1]

Import commitments by domestic buyers for the next few years as of January 1, 1976, are shown in table 8-1. The amount of uranium that can be imported from other countries depends greatly on the foreign requirements of uranium, world uranium prices, and the regulatory policies of the uranium-exporting countries.

A great deal of uranium for which arrangements have not been made so far may come from foreign countries. The amount of unfilled requirements, based on the nuclear capacity in operation, under construction, and planned as of January 1, 1976, is shown in table 8-2. The chances of procuring uranium from other countries also depend to a great extent on the requirements and production capabilities of those countries.

The information provided in table 8-2 is for the period 1977-1990. This information indicates the amount of uranium that should come in some proportions from domestic production and from foreign imports. The analysis in the following chapters forecasts the market supply of uranium production for certain postulated nuclear capacity forecasts. If the uranium requirements are higher than output forecasts in the model simulation, one can then determine the approximate amount that can be imported from abroad. However, if the world price is far lower than the forecasted price for U.S. uranium, the imports will be much higher than shown in this study. Similarly, if the world prices are

Table 8-1
Import Commitments by Domestic Buyers, 1975-1990
(tons of U_3O_8)

Year of U_3O_8 Delivery	Annual	Cumulative
1975	1100	1,100
1976	2900	4,000
1977	4000	8,000
1978	2600	10,600
1979	3300	13,900
1980	4200	18,100
1981	4300	22,400
1982	4100	26,500
1983	4100	30,600
1984	3800	34,400
1985	3500	37,900
1986	2500	40,400
1987-1990	1800/year	47,200

Source: Energy Research and Development Administration, *Survey of United States Uranium Marketing Activity*, ERDA-77-46, May 1977, p. 12.

Table 8-2
Unfilled Uranium Requirements, 1977-1990

Year	Tons of U_3O_8	Year	Tons of U_3O_8
1977	1,100	1984	15,900
1978	1,400	1985	18,200
1979	3,500	1986	22,800
1980	5,100	1987	26,900
1981	7,300	1988	27,400
1982	11,200	1989	30,700
1983	14,800	1990	30,400

Source: Energy Research and Development Administration, *Survey of United States Uranium Marketing Activity*, ERDA-77-46, May 1977, p. 16.

higher than the forecasts for U.S. uranium, then imports will be lesser in amount and the higher world price will stimulate domestic production. In this case the domestic output forecasts will be much higher for domestic use than has been shown in the model. If there are no governmental restrictions, exports of uranium will increase.

Uranium Exports

There have been very small amounts of uranium exports, and there may be small amounts after 1980. The present commitments by domestic producers for uranium sales are shown in table 8-3. The cumulative uranium exports will reach a level of 13,500 tons of U_3O_8 by 1990. These are relatively smaller than the anticipated imports for the United States.

Table 8-3
Uranium Exports to Foreign Countries, 1976-1990 (Commitments as of January 1, 1977)

Year of Delivery	Tons of U_3O_8 Annual	Cumulative
1966-1975	–	7,400
1976	600	8,000
1977	2,100	10,100
1978	900	11,000
1979	900	11,900
1980-1990	1,600	13,500

Source: Energy Research and Development Administration, *Survey of United States Uranium Marketing Activity*, ERDA-77-46, May 1977, p. 12.

Table 8-4
Inventory Held by Domestic Buyers, 1971–1976

Year	Tons of U_3O_8
1971	7,200
1972	14,400
1973	20,000
1974	20,200
1975	22,600
1976	25,800

Uranium Inventory

The amount of inventory carried by buyers over a period of time is shown in table 8-4. The 1976 inventory shown here is equal to twice the amount of uranium mined in the year 1976. Since the minimum time lag between buying the uranium and using it as a fuel in the reactor is approximately two years, the inventory size is considered reasonable. Uranium buyers include the utilities, agents, and reactor manufacturers. An inventory of uranium is also carried by the uranium producers; it happened to be a relatively smaller quantity in January 1977 than in previous years, 2,300 tons of U_3O_8.[2] The amount of inventory that will be carried by buyers depends on their attitudes. They could be either risk averse or risk takers with regard to the future supplies. Buyers also weigh the economic costs associated with carrying inventory over the required margin against the risk of running short in the supply of fuel.

Notes

1. Energy Research and Development Administration, *U.S. Nuclear Power Export Activities, Final Environmental Statement,* Report 1542, vol. 1, April 1976, pp. 3–37; idem, *Nuclear Fuel Cycle Report by the Fuel Cycle Task Force,* ERDA-33, March 1975, p. 14.
2. Energy Research and Development Administration, *Survey of United States Uranium Marketing Activity,* ERDA-76-46, April 1976, p. 15.

9 Forecasts of Energy

Energy is an essential ingredient in economic growth. Higher per capita energy consumption has often been associated with higher levels of per capita income for different countries of the world. The historical pattern of U.S. energy consumption, which shows enormous use of energy, should not be construed as "wasteful" or "sinful." The choice of developing energy-intensive processes in the structure of the American economy was purely an economic one that replaced mundane, routine, and labor-intensive methods of production. As has been the case, rising energy costs will initiate a mechanism in the economic system that will determine the optimal allocation of energy in relation to capital, labor, and other scarce resources.

The forecasts of the future requirements of total energy, electric energy, and nuclear electric energy are discussed in relation to the various developments that have taken place in the last few years.

Demand for Total Energy

The demand for total energy is determined by the decisions of numerous consumers in a given period of time. These decisions are influenced by fuel prices, income, technology, and various other economic and noneconomic factors. Future demand for energy is generally linked to future trends in the growth rates of an economy. The alternative projections of energy demand reflect the effects of economic, environmental, and institutional factors. An econometric study of the U.S. energy future by Data Resources, Inc. (DRI), predicts that economic growth between 1975 and 2000 will be within the range of 3.5 percent to 3.4 percent per year in the GNP. Based on these assumptions, the DRI study predicts energy growth to fall within the range of 3.1 percent to 2.3 percent per year.[1] Using the DRI model, the Congressional Research Service projects that annual energy growth rates will vary between 2.5 percent and 3.1 percent per year.[2] A more recent work on nuclear studies states that the U.S. economy will grow at a much slower rate, as low as 2.5 percent, and that the demand for energy will increase at the rate of 1.5 percent per year.[3]

Figure 9-1 shows the various projections of energy demand. Implicit in the forecasts are future developments concerning energy resources, energy prices, and government policies affecting future energy use. These forecasts of energy demand vary from a high of 190Q–195Q to a low of 100Q in the year 2000.

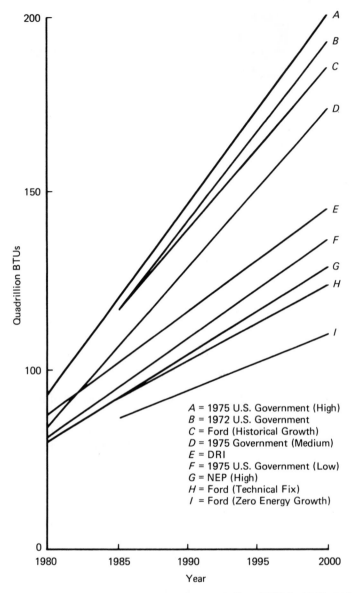

Figure 9-1. Total Energy Forecasts (in quadrillion BTUs), 1980–2000

The 1975 U.S. official estimates of three scenarios (high, medium, low) represent effects of different policies on energy demand. The high-growth scenario represents the ongoing trend of low energy prices with no concern for energy conservation. The medium-growth energy scenario shows the reduction in energy demand resulting from increasing energy prices and the efforts to conserve energy. The low-growth scenario represents a situation in which energy conservation is predominant in affecting the future energy use. The Ford policy project considers three possible energy scenarios, historical growth, technical fix, and zero energy growth, in the evaluation of alternate energy strategies for the U.S. economy.[4] Historical growth is identified with the continuing pattern of energy use at the rate of 3.4 percent per year. The technical fix scenario emphasizes conservation in the energy strategy and slower economic growth. The zero energy growth requires several structural changes in the economy for achieving greater energy efficiency. The national energy plan formulates future energy demand to be 93Q in 1985 and 124Q in 2000.[5] Such a reduction in energy demand is to be achieved by a series of economic measures that will be adopted by the government.

It is unlikely that either the high- or the low-energy demand case in figure 9-1 will be realized by the year 2000. The present economic and energy policies make the medium case, especially the national energy plan, the more likely energy future of the U.S. economy in the year 2000.

Electric Energy Demand

Electric power generation and consumption trends have shown rapid increases over the last hundred years. The oil embargo in 1973, fears of energy shortages, and increasing conservation measures have slowed electric energy growth for the last few years. But the consumption of electricity, during the years 1975–2000, is expected to increase at the rate of 5 percent per year.[6] Future increases in electric energy consumption are projected to result from the possible constancy of real prices of electricity. The increased use of electricity is also likely to come from its possible substitution for other fuels as other fuels become relatively expensive.[7]

The electric energy is produced by nuclear, coal, oil, gas, and hydro. The major future sources of energy for producing electricity are coal and nuclear fuels. The amount of gas used in electricity generation (utility) was approximately 14 percent of the total natural gas supplies in 1960, 15 percent in 1965, and 18 percent in 1971.[8] Of the total electricity generated, approximately 20 percent was from natural gas in 1960 and about 24 percent in 1971. More recently there has been a rapid decline in the percentage of gas used in electricity production. In the future, on the basis of Federal Power Commission orders, natural gas will not be used in new plants, and its use in older plants will be phased out or modified whenever alternatives are available. Higher gas prices and uncertain gas supplies will drive the electric industry toward coal and nuclear fuel.[9]

In 1977 coal accounted for 46.9 percent of the total electric generation followed by oil, nuclear, gas, and hydro.[10] Nuclear accounted for 13 percent of the total electric generation in 1977 and was estimated to increase to approximately 28 percent by 1985. A remarkable change in the relative contribution of alternative fuels is expected to take place in the use of gas as a fuel for electric power production. Gas currently accounts for 12 percent, and its relative share is expected to decline to a low of 2.8 percent in 1986.[11] Beyond 1986 nuclear and coal will remain the major fuels for electric power production.

The relative market share of nuclear energy depends on the relative economic attractiveness of nuclear plants as well as their environmental and social acceptability. Nuclear plants are capital intensive but appear to have economic superiority over coal plants because of projected lower fuel costs. There has been a great deal of speculation about whether the rising uranium prices, which will manifest themselves in higher fuel costs, will weaken the economic competitiveness of nuclear plants.

The present economic status of electric generation is such that nuclear plants have an economic advantage over coal plants with and without scrubbers. The economic choice for nuclear can shift to coal only if nuclear costs double due to rapid increases in uranium prices or to a decline in the real prices of coal.[12]

The demand for electric energy is generally expressed as a function of population growth, income, population of electricity consumers, and sales of consumer goods that use electric energy. One such formulation of energy demand is given as[13]

$$EE = f(P_e, \bar{Y}, N) \tag{9.1}$$

where

EE = electricity consumption

P_e = electricity price

$\bar{Y}$ = per capita income

N = population

and the demand for electric energy capacity is expressed as

$$Q = f(k, FC, E) \tag{9.2}$$

where

Q = total installed electric energy capacity

k = capital price

FC = fuel cost

E = forecasted change in EE

Allowing for the fact that the stock of generating equipment must be maintained by replacement, along with the incremental demands for new capacity, one can express total demand for electric energy capacity as

$$Q = f(k, FC, E, \alpha KC) \tag{9.3}$$

where α represents the depreciation rate of the capital stock KC, which has been accumulated over a period of time. Electric energy capacity includes coal as well

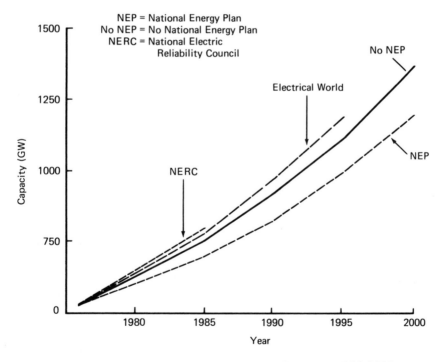

Figure 9-2. Total Electric Energy Capacity Forecasts, 1975–2000

as nuclear, and the relative share going to nuclear capacity depends on the relative prices of capital and fuel:[14]

$$Q_n/Q = F(k_n, FC_n, k_f, FC_f) \qquad (9.4)$$

where the subscripts n and f denote nuclear and fossil.

The forecasts of electricity consumption made by different authors for the year 2000 differ widely based on different assumptions. These forecasts range from a low of 2.01 trillion to a high of 10.25 trillion kilowatt-hours of electricity consumption in the year 2000.[15] The current forecasts for electric capacity are provided in figure 9-2. The future trends in total electric energy capacity are important in the study of demand for nuclear electric and for uranium. The total electric energy, according to the national energy plan, is projected to be 1,200 GW. Failure of coal to provide its own share of electricity will place greater burdens on the nuclear industry. It is therefore essential to consider the relative share of nuclear and coal in the economic evaluation of total energy systems.

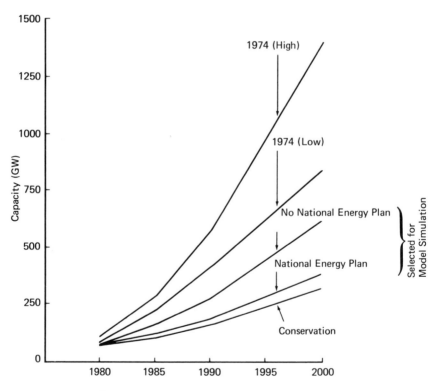

Figure 9-3. Nuclear Capacity Forecasts, 1975-2000

Nuclear Capacity Forecasts

The forecasts of nuclear capacity are important in the analysis of uranium demand. Several studies have forecasted electricity growth and the nuclear share of the market.[16] These forecasts have frequently been revised downward, as with the case of forecasts for total energy and electric energy. The official estimates prepared by the Energy Research and Development Administration (ERDA) in late 1974 postulate several scenarios, ranging from a low forecast of 850 GW to a high of 1,400 GW of nuclear capacity in 2000 (figure 9-3). An interesting feature of these forecasts is that as late as 1974 the majority of the estimates were above 1,000 GW of nuclear capacity for the year 2000. Revised forecasts in mid 1975 by ERDA show a further decline in the future nuclear capacity growth.[17] The current estimates of the nuclear capacity forecasts as formulated in the national energy plan show a considerable reduction from the previous one. The conservation scenario depicts the situation in which the government is successful in achieving the goal of conservation in energy use. The 1977 forecasts, shown in figure 9-3, have been used in the model simulation for forecasting price.

Notes

1. E.A. Hudson and D.W. Jorgenson, "Tax Policy and Energy Conservation," in *Econometric Studies of U.S. Energy Policy,* ed. D.W. Jorgenson, North-Holland, Amsterdam, 1976, pp. 44-60.

2. *Project Interdependence: U.S. and World Energy Outlook Through 1990,* Congressional Research Service, Committee on Natural Resources, Library of Congress, November 1977, pp. 263-300.

3. H.A. Feiveson et al., "An Evolutionary Strategy for Nuclear Power: Alternatives to Breeders," unpublished report, Program on Nuclear Policy Alternatives, Center for Environmental Studies, Princeton University, Princeton, N.J., June 1978.

4. The Ford Foundation Energy Policy Project, *A Time to Choose: America's Energy Future,* Ballinger Publishing Company, Cambridge, Mass., 1974.

5. The factors that will help realize the goal of 93Q energy demand in 1985 in the national energy plan are projected for the remaining period of fifteen years to get to a total of 124Q in 2000 by R.W. Bowen and R.H. Williamson, "Domestic Uranium Requirements," paper presented at Uranium Industry Seminar, GJO, October 1977, p.3.

6. Hudson and Jorgensen, "Tax Policy," p. 58.

7. Ibid., p. 53.

8. U.S. Department of the Interior, Bureau of Mines, *Supply and Demand for Energy in the United States by States and Regions, 1960 and 1965,* 1975.

9. U.S. Department of the Interior, *United States Energy Fact Sheets,* February 1973; U.S. Department of the Interior, Bureau of Mines, *Fuels and Energy Data, United States and Regions,* Information Circular 974, 1972.

10. National Electric Reliability Council, *Annual Review,* July 1977, p. 9.

11. Ibid., p. 9.

12. Comptroller General of the United States, U.S. Coal Development: Priorities, Uncertainties, September 22, 1977, pp. 2-45.

13. This formulation of energy demand was proposed by Paul MacAvoy. See P. MacAvoy, *Economic Strategy for Developing Nuclear Breeder Reactors,* MIT Press, Cambridge, Mass., 1969; for alternative formulations of the demand for energy, see Hudson and Jorgensen, "Tax Policy."

14. For a detailed formulation of the problem and model simulation, see MacAvoy, *Economic Strategy.*

15. Hudson and Jorgenson, *Econometric Studies of U.S. Energy Policy,* North-Holland, Amsterdam, 1976, p. 62; see also National Electric Reliability Council, *Annual Review,* July 1977.

16. P.N. Ross, "The Nuclear Electric Company," paper presented at Westinghouse Electric Corporation Conference on Hydrogen Economy, June 1973; Ford Foundation, "A Time to Choose; America's Energy Future," Final Report of the Energy Policy Project, 1974; National Academy of Engineering, "U.S. Energy Prospects: An Engineering Viewpoint," Washington, D.C., 1974; Federal Energy Administration, "Project Independence Report," Washington, D.C., 1974; Energy Research and Development Administration, *Nuclear Power Growth 1974-2000,* WASH-1139 (1974); ERDA Office of Planning and Analysis, "Total Energy, Electric Energy, and Nuclear Power Projections, United States," February 1975; ERDA, *A National Plan for Energy Research, Development, and Demonstration; Creating Energy Choices for the Future,* ERDA-48 (June 1975); Paul Jaskow and M. Baughman, "The Future of the U.S. Nuclear Energy Industry," *Bell J. Econ.* 7 (1976):3-32.

17. ERDA, *National Plan,* ERDA-48, p. 42.

10 Demand for Uranium

The cumulative requirements of uranium are generally calculated on the basis of future expected nuclear capacity. The amount of uranium required also depends on certain technological factors that occur in the nuclear industry. For example, alternative enrichment tails assay requirements, plutonium recycling, and the application of laser technology for isotope separation can considerably alter the demand for uranium.

A distinction is made between the demand for uranium and the requirements of uranium. The demand for uranium is defined as a function of the uranium price and of the other relevant economic variables, whereas the requirements of uranium are calculated for alternative nuclear capacity forecasts under various assumptions relating to uranium recycling and tails assay. This study assumes that the lightwater reactors, pressurized water reactors and boiling water reactors, will continue to dominate the nuclear industry until the end of this century. Beyond the year 2000 the nuclear industry can pursue various options for reactor designs and fuel cycles in its expansion of nuclear programs.

Certain alternative uranium-conserving fuel cycles have been proposed as a continuation of the present lightwater reactor programs. The Canadian heavy water reactors, which are considered uranium efficient, may find their way in the U.S. and world nuclear industries. The entry of alternative, proliferation-resistant reactor designs in the nuclear industry and their effects on the uranium requirements can be felt only after a long time.[1] The implications of such nuclear alternatives on uranium demand are not considered here.

Uranium Requirements

The lifetime needs, thirty years, of a 1,000–MW nuclear reactor are estimated to be in the range of 4,000 to 6,000 tons of U_3O_8. Once a decision to build the nuclear plant is made, the electric utility enters the uranium market to seek the uranium supplies for meeting the fuel needs of the initial core loading. A decision to procure additional supplies of uranium is influenced primarily by the current market prices of uranium and by the expectations concerning the future uranium prices. The time and size of the uranium purchases are constrained by the utilities' levels of inventories and by their enrichment contracts with the ERDA plants.

The uranium marketing and procurement activity for the United States is published annually by the Energy Research and Development Administration (ERDA) in the report, *Survey of U.S. Uranium Marketing Activity,* which in 1976 covered seventy utilities, five reactor manufacturers, and thirty-eight uranium producers.[2] The cumulative uranium requirements for a nuclear generating capacity of 203 GW are estimated to be approximately 450 thousand tons of U_3O_8 in the year 1990. These estimates are derived by ERDA on the basis of 0.2 percent enrichment tails assay requirements until the year 1980; tails are then increased to 0.25 percent. It was assumed that there will be no plutonium recycling, in compliance with the present official policy.

The difference between the cumulative uranium requirements and the cumulative delivery commitments gives the information concerning the amount of uranium that should be procured during the period 1977–1990 in order to cover the future fuel needs of the projected nuclear capacity. The cumulative delivery commitments, domestic and foreign, and the inventories held by the buyers are more than sufficient to meet the requirements of the projected nuclear capacity until 1983. The cumulative requirements for 1983 are estimated to be 175 thousand tons of U_3O_8. The uranium needs for the next seven years, 1983 to 1990, are said to be around 233 thousand tons, which should come from either the domestic or foreign markets. Uranium supply arrangements are generally made through different sources. Purchases may be made directly from primary producers of yellowcake, from fuel manufacturers, from agents, and from ERDA leases. The relative share of uranium supply coming from the domestic reactor manufacturer is very small and will be negligible in the future. The participation of the reactor manufacturers in the uranium market is likely to be limited in the future, especially after the Westinghouse litigations with the electric utilities.

Uranium Demand

The total demand for uranium is defined to consist of the following categories:

$$Q_t^d = \sum_{i=1}^{3} q_{it}^d$$

where

Q_t^d = total quantity of uranium demanded at time t

q_{1t}^d = demand for uranium from nuclear capacity in operation at time t

q_{2t}^d = demand for uranium from nuclear capacity under construction at time t

q_{3t}^d = demand for uranium from nuclear capacity on order at time t

The demand for uranium can be divided into short-term demand and long-term demand. Short-term demand may be defined as the quantity of uranium needed to fuel the reactors already in operation and under construction. Unless the plants in operation are shut down permanently, the lifetime uranium requirements of these plants must be met. It is logical to assume that the short-term demand is price inelastic and will become highly so as time progresses. The demand for uranium for reactors under construction is well defined. Price increases will have some effects and may lead to deferrals of the plants under construction, but they will not affect the long-term demand. The demand curve for the plants in operation and for the ones under construction may resemble those shown in figure 10-1a. The curve dd indicates responsiveness of demand with respect to price. This curve applies to a situation in which the nuclear plants are in operation and under construction and the utilities have made some arrangements for the first reloads of the operation. The utilities are willing to buy more and more uranium at lower prices. The quantity of uranium needed is known here, but the time and the order size is not known with certainty. However, this situation gradually changes as the utilities can no longer delay the procurement of uranium to fuel the reactors. In this situation the demand curve becomes progressively inelastic $(d'd')$ and finally becomes perfectly inelastic $(d''d'')$. This curve denotes a situation in which the utility must either buy the quantity $0q''$ at any price or shut down the plant.

The long-term demand includes the demand potential from the reactors of the first two categories as well as the demand from the reactors on order. The aggregate demand can be characterized as relatively price elastic. The increases and decreases in uranium prices in the long run will generate lower or higher demands for uranium. The demand potential of the reactors on order may not

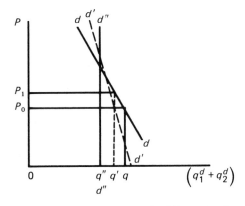

Figure 10-1. Short-term Uranium Demand for Plants in Operation and under Construction

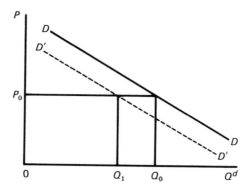

Figure 10–2. Long-Run Demand Curves for Uranium

be fulfilled, because they may be deferred or canceled, depending on the electricity demand and the expected relative capital and fuel costs of alternative energy sources. The curve *DD* in figure 10-2 reflects the aggregate demand for uranium, which includes the demand potential for the reactors on order. In the long run the rapid increases in prices may cause some utilities to cancel the reactor orders and to explore the possibilities of substitution by coal plants. Such a development will shift the demand curve downward to *D'D'* and reduce the quantity demand from $0Q_0$ to $0Q_1$. In the same manner the increasing coal prices may cause the utilities to shift toward nuclear plants and in the long run cause an increase in the demand for uranium.

Modeling the Demand Side

The demand for uranium by electric utilities is defined as a function of uranium prices and the prices of alternative fuels. Inclusion of the prices of gas and oil may seem appropriate, but in the future it is only the price of coal that is directly relevant and competitive with nuclear fuel prices in electricity generation. Gas and oil should no longer be considered direct substitutes for nuclear fuel. However, the world price of oil does have an influence on the price of all other energy sources. Therefore the world price of oil is treated as an independent variable along with the price of coal. Another variable of significance in the analysis is the expectation concerning the capital prices for nuclear fuel and for coal. It has not been possible to include the capital prices for coal and nuclear in the demand equation because of the lack of reliable and sufficient data for this variable. The demand equation is therefore expressed as

$$Q_t^d = \alpha + \beta_1 \log NCP_{t-1} + \beta_2 \log PC_{t-1} + \beta_3 \log WPO_{t-1} + \beta_4 \log PU_{t-1} \tag{10.1}$$

where

    NCP = cumulative nuclear capacity

     PC = price of coal

   WPO = world price of oil

This relationship is formulated on the assumption that the prices of coal will affect the demand for uranium in the long run. Equation 10.1 has not been estimated here, but it has been used in the derivation of a reduced form of the price equation. In many industry studies the demand for the product is the central part of economic analysis. In the case of uranium the demand analysis is inconsequential, because the price of uranium represents a very small proportion of the total cost of electricity generated.

An alternate specification of the demand equation is to relate the quantity of uranium required as a function of the cumulative nuclear capacity. This relationship should be viewed as an engineering and technical relationship. Assuming that the quantity of uranium demanded is equal to the quantity of uranium supplied, the price equation can then be estimated as a function of the level of uranium reserves and the quantity of uranium demanded. This type of formulation has been discussed further in the analysis of uranium prices.

Notes

1. F. Von Hippel, "Alternative Uranium-Conserving, Proliferation-Resistant Fuel Cycles: Some Preliminary Results," unpublished report, Center for Environmental Studies, Princeton University, Princeton, N.J., December 10, 1977; for a detailed description of isotopic denatured fuel cycles, see H.A. Feiveson et al., "An Evolutionary Strategy for Nuclear Power," Program on Nuclear Policy Alternatives, Center for Environmental Studies, Princeton University, Princeton, N.J., June 1978.

2. J.A. Patterson and G.F. Combs, "Uranium Market Activities," unpublished report, U.S. Department of Energy, Washington, D.C., October 1977.

11 History of Uranium Prices

In a market economy prices regulate production and consumption activities and ensure the allocative efficiency of scarce resources. For prices to be effective regulators, there must exist a competitive market structure, and several other assumptions must be satisfied. The history of uranium prices shows an interesting trend of government-fixed prices compared with the prices determined by supply and demand.

Government-Administered Prices

The initial buying program of the Atomic Energy Commission (AEC) involved arrangements that guaranteed markets and prices for uranium ore and uranium concentrate. The uranium prices paid by the AEC varied from time to time. The AEC used two main approaches in the pricing of uranium ore and concentrate. The first method refers to guaranteed ore prices, which included payment for both uranium and vanadium. Bonuses were offered for the discovery of new mines. The price of uranium concentrate was negotiated with the milling companies on the basis of guaranteed ore prices, transportation and ore-milling costs, and amortization of the capital costs of the plant. This pricing method was used until 1962.

In 1948 and 1949 Circulars 3 and 4 issued by the AEC fixed the base price per ton of ore and the price per pound of uranium on the basis of the percentage of uranium content. These circulars describe in detail the cost breakdown and the price composition for different grades of ore. The base price per ton of ore was fixed at \$0.60 for 0.10 percent U_3O_8 and rose gradually to \$60 per ton for ores containing 2.00 percent U_3O_8. The base price included additional payments for the development allowance, premium, and facilities allowance for ores containing 0.25 percent U_3O_8 or more in a ton of ore. The price schedules were further revised, and Circulars 5 and 5 (revised) were issued. The base price of low-grade ores was increased. Soon after Circular 5 (revised) was issued, Circular 6 was issued in 1951 which added a production bonus for the delivery of each 10,000 pounds of uranium. This order further increased the base price per pound of uranium to \$3.50 and \$7.50 for ores containing 0.10 and 0.20 percent of U_3O_8 respectively. In all these price schedules the AEC's intention appeared to be to set the price equivalent to the competitive market prices. It is important to this study to know whether there would have been any significant differences between the prices fixed by AEC and the competitive market prices that would have prevailed in the absence of government intervention.

A brief survey of the price formation in the uranium-mining industry shows that substantial profits were earned by the producers on their investments in uranium exploration, mining, and milling operations. This conclusion has been drawn on the basis of the AEC's practices in the determination of production costs, which allowed a substantial margin for the recovery of profits on capital investments.[1] The trend in the price increase continued until 1953. During this period the prices reached a high of $12 per pound in the mid 1950s. This price level provided an incentive for increasing exploration and for technological improvements, which ultimately reduced the uranium prices to a low level of $8 per pound of U_3O_8 in the late 1950s and the early 1960s.

Another approach used by the AEC was the stretchout program in the middle 1960s. For the period 1962–1968 the price of concentrate was fixed at $8 per pound. The deliveries scheduled for the period 1963–1966 were stretched to a period through 1968. As a consequence of the stretchout program, some of the uranium purchases originally planned for 1967 and 1968 were deferred until 1969 and 1970. The prices paid for the ore bought in 1969 and 1970, including the deferred quantity, were determined on the basis of a formula that allowed 85 percent of the unit production costs plus $1.60, the total not to exceed $6.70. The average price paid by the AEC during 1969 and 1970 was estimated at $5.78. This price was not favorable for industry expansion, because the prices did not include items such as interest costs, depreciation of mill facilities, and some overhead costs.[2]

Prices in Private Markets

In 1968 private industry began to participate in the procurement of uranium ore along with the government. However, delays in plant construction and operation schedules and some cancellations of nuclear plants led to changes in delivery schedules and commitments. As a result, there was a buildup of inventory and slack in the industry's production and capacity growth. The low prices continued to prevail in the uranium markets, with a price range from $5.00 to $5.50 per pound of U_3O_8. In 1971 the prices for immediate delivery reached a low of $4.00 per pound of U_3O_8.

The situation was different in 1973 when the nuclear utility industry aggressively sought uranium. The oil embargo and the fears of energy shortages resulted in the utilities' seeking U_3O_8 in amounts as great as 150,000 tons in 1973, including future deliveries to 1990. This excess demand generated upward pressures on prices, especially because of the industry's inability to expand short-run production to meet future requirements. The result was a sharp in-

Table 11-1
Uranium Prices in Private Markets, 1970-1976
(dollars per pound of U_3O_8)

Year	Average Price[a]
1970	6.30
1971	6.20
1972	6.30
1973	6.50
1974	8.30
1975	12.30
1976	16.25

Source: Electric Power Research Institute, *Uranium Price Formation,* EA-498, October 1977, p. 9-43. Reprinted with permission.

[a]Prices reported here are the weighted average of the immediate and long-term contract prices.

crease in the prices for immediate as well as future delivery of uranium. The prices for immediate delivery reached a high of $15 per pound in 1974 and $27 per pound in 1975. In the midst of these interesting developments, which provided a big push to the uranium industry, certain unexpected happenings created a great deal of uncertainty in the uranium market. In July 1975 Westinghouse announced its unwillingness to honor its commitment to supply 65 million pounds of uranium to the electric utilities. The market price of uranium at that time was $26 per pound, but Westinghouse was committed to supply uranium at a price of $8 to $9 per pound of U_3O_8. Seeking a legal refuge under the Uniform Commercial Code, Westinghouse withdrew the offer. The legal battles among the electric utilities, the producers, and the oil companies raged for a long time. The impact on the uranium market has not been assessed here.

Since 1973, uranium price data have been collected from uranium buyers and published periodically by the AEC. The results of these surveys reveal the future trends in uranium prices. The average uranium prices in private markets for the years 1970-1976 are shown in table 11-1.

Future Uranium Prices

The price formation reported by the Department of Energy includes the uranium procurements by different methods. There are primarily three price arrangements by which future delivery of uranium is procured. The majority of the commitments are based on the "contract prices." The contract prices are defined as the prices determined by the terms of the contract entered into by the buyer and the seller. Such a contract may include a clause for future escalations

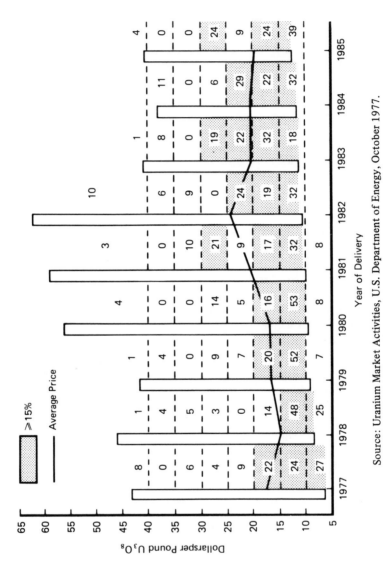

Figure 11-1. Average Price Trend 1977–1985 (Reported U_3O_8 Prices as of July 1, 1977)

Source: Uranium Market Activities, U.S. Department of Energy, October 1977.

of prices based on various economic indices. In the "market price" contract the price for uranium at the time of delivery is determined by the prevalent market price at or before the time of delivery. In the "other" price contract the price is determined on a cost-plus basis. It has recently become common practice for the electric utilities to enter the uranium markets in order to procure uranium supplies for future nuclear plants. In such a case the price of uranium represents the production costs which will include the opportunity cost of the capital. As of July 1, 1977, the average prices for future delivery were well below $20 per pound of U_3O_8 for the years 1977-1981. The average future price shows a modest increase in 1982 and then a decline to $20 per pound for the years 1984 and 1985. Figure 11-1 shows that a relatively smaller proportion of the uranium was bought at very high prices for future uranium delivery. As buyers enter into new contracts at higher prices for the future delivery of uranium, the average prices for the years 1978-1985 will increase. The extent of future increases in price depends on the pressures that will be generated by excess demand for filling the required amounts of uranium for the reactors in operation and under construction. In addition, the average prices will increase as the old contracts are retired or renegotiated at higher prices. The "average prices" shown in figure 11-1 will also serve the purpose of comparing the reliability of price forecasts made in this study. The reasons for any differences in the present average prices and the price forecasts are explained in a later chapter.

Notes

1. Electric Power Research Institute, *Uranium Price Formation,* EA-498, October 1977, pp. 9-1 to 9-61.

2. Supplemental Testimony of J.A. Patterson, in the matter of Kansas Gas and Electric Company and Kansas City Power and Light Company, before the Atomic Safety and Licensing Board, Nuclear Regulatory Commission, Wolf Creek, Docket No. STN-50-482, July 1976.

12 Uranium Price Analysis

Uranium price analysis can be viewed as an initial exploratory effort in explaining the process of uranium price formation. The predictive ability of the price equation is more important to the present study than its ramifications of theoretical construct in the domain of economic analysis.

Approaches to Price Formation

Economic analysis of the demand and supply of a commodity reflecting the adjustment process can be modeled in many different ways.[1] One such approach is the Marshallian approach in which the supply prices PU^s and the demand prices PU^d are given as functions on the quantity demanded and supplied:

$$PU^s = f(q), \quad PU^d = f(q)$$

Another approach is Walrasian, in which the supply and demand are defined as a function of commodity price:

$$q^s = f(PU), \quad q^d = f(PU)$$

One needs to assume that the uranium price is set for each period and that change in the uranium price from one period to another occurs in response to the excess supply or excess demand of the earlier period. The price increases if there is an increase in the excess demand and decreases when there is excess supply. The price adjustment equation can then be shown as

$$\Delta PU_t = \Psi(q^d_{t-1} - q^s_{t-1})$$
$$= \Psi[d(PU_{t-1}) - s(PU_{t-1})]$$

The price does not change when $q^s_t = q^d_t$. The deviation from the equation price P may be written $\bar{P} = P - P^e$. The incremental equation price can be reduced as follows.

$$q^s = \alpha_0 + \alpha_1(P - P^e) = \alpha_0 + \alpha_1\bar{P}$$
$$q^d = \beta_0 + \beta_1(P - P^e) = \beta_0 + \beta_1\bar{P}$$

Then

$$\Delta \bar{P} = \gamma(q_{t-1}^d - q_{t-1}^s)$$
$$= \gamma(\beta_0 + \beta_1 \bar{P}_{t-1} - \alpha_0 - \alpha_1 \bar{P}_{t-1})$$
$$= \gamma(\beta_1 - \alpha_1)\bar{P}_{t-1}$$

The adjustment process in the Marshallian approach requires that the available quantity be considered set for each time period. The available quantity in the following period is said to increase or decrease depending on the supply and demand price of the product.

$$\Delta q = \phi(P_{t-1}^d - P_{t-1}^s)$$

In the real world prices and quantities are not determined simultaneously; instead there is a recursive relationship between demand and supply. Wold[2] suggested an adjustment process that is more realistic and more applicable to the field of resources. According to Wold, the sellers set the prices, and buyers then react and make their appropriate decisions which in turn serve as inputs to the sellers' reactions. In the uranium-mining industry there exists a definite recursive relationship between prices and supply. The relationship, however, is in reverse order compared with Wold's suggestion of adjustment process in the resource industry. In uranium mining the sellers react to market prices and make appropriate decisions concerning the supply of uranium reserves and production. The level of reserves, along with the decisions made by the buyers, in turn, determines the current market prices.

Uranium Price Equation

A detailed description of the industry behavior from the previous chapter provides a rational basis for deriving the reserve, supply, and demand equations. Equations 12.1 and 12.2 were formulated in an earlier chapter.

$$\log q_t^s = \alpha_0 + \alpha_1 \log RR_{t-1} + \alpha_2 \log PU_{t-1} \qquad (12.1)$$

$$\log q_t^d = \gamma_0 + \gamma_1 \log NCP_{t-1} + \gamma_2 \log PC_{t-1}$$
$$+ \gamma_3 \log WPO_{t-1} + \gamma_4 \log PU_{t-1} \qquad (12.2)$$

Equations 12.1 and 12.2 were then set as equal to obtain the price equation.

$$\log PU_{t-1} = \frac{(\gamma_0 - \alpha_0)}{(\alpha_2 - \gamma_4)} + (\alpha_1/\alpha_2 - \gamma_4) \log RR_{t-1}$$

$$+ (\gamma_1/\alpha_2 - \gamma_4) \log NCP_{t-1}$$

$$+ (\gamma_2/\alpha_2 - \gamma_4) \log PC_{t-1} \qquad (12.3)$$

$$+ (\gamma_3/\alpha_2 - \gamma_4) \log WPO_{t-1}$$

This equation is then expressed as

$$\log PU_t = \alpha + \beta_1 \log RR_t + \beta_2 \log NCP_t$$

$$+ \beta_3 \log PC_t + \beta_4 \log WPO_t \qquad (12.4)$$

Equation 12.4 reflects the effects of supply and demand for uranium in determining the uranium prices. The term RR involving uranium reserves reflects the effects of supply. The terms involving the prices of coal PC and oil WPO and the nuclear capacity NCP represent the effects of demand on future uranium prices. The underlying relationship between prices and the reserves-supply relationship is simple and is shown in the following figure.

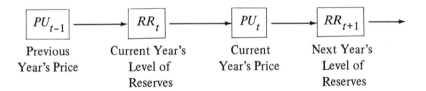

PU_{t-1}	RR_t	PU_t	RR_{t+1}
Previous Year's Price	Current Year's Level of Reserves	Current Year's Price	Next Year's Level of Reserves

In the estimation of the price equation (12.4), the effect of government intervention in the uranium market on the supply side became an issue concerning the proper use of the time series data. The government fixed the prices in the uranium markets until 1968. The period 1968-1970 shows mixed participation by the government and private industry in the uranium industry. Since 1970, private industry has been the sole buyer of uranium. Equation 12.4 has been estimated for the period 1965-1975, which includes the four years of government intervention in the private markets. This time period was selected because the nuclear capacity appeared as a competitive source of electric power beginning in 1965. The Chow test was used to determine whether the econometric estimates with and without the government intervention in the market were different for the periods 1959-1975 and 1968-1975.[3] The test shows that the statistical estimate of the two samples were not different and that the pooling of the two samples was warranted.

Alternate Price Formulation

Various alternative formulations that can be derived emphasize the different aspects of the supply and demand for uranium. With the assumption that the world price of oil is irrelevant to the explanation of future uranium price formation, equation 12.4 can be estimated without the variable WPO. Another logical explanation of future prices can be derived by considering the effect of the previous year's uranium prices on current prices and by excluding the price of oil and nuclear capacity from the model. The relationship then becomes

$$\log Pu_t = \alpha + \beta_1 \log RR_t + \beta_2 \log PC_t + \beta_3 \log PU_{t-1}$$

Therefore there are numerous alternate formulations of the model.

Perl defines the uranium price to be a function of the extraction costs of the uranium. The equilibrium price, in the long run, is assumed to be equal to the marginal extraction cost of the uranium reserves. These costs include the costs of exploration, discovery, and extraction of the incremental reserves to meet the demand. The study by Perl uses the following equation in estimating uranium prices for alternative levels of uranium demand.[4]

$$P = \left\{ \left(\frac{RD}{\alpha_0 e^{T\alpha_3}} \right)^{\frac{\beta_1}{\alpha_1}} e^{T\beta_2} \gamma_1 \lambda (\alpha_2 + 1) \beta_0 \right\}^{\frac{\alpha_1}{\alpha_2 \beta_1 + \alpha_1}}$$

where P refers to price, RD is the discovery of reserves, and λ is the adjustment factor to convert the extraction costs into selling price. The variable T refers to the time period. A unique feature of this approach is that the cumulative uranium requirements are calculated for alternative nuclear growth scenarios and the prices are then determined for supplying the required amounts of uranium. The major assumption in this case is that all the uranium requirements of the projected nuclear capacity are met from the domestic uranium production. This assumption is not plausible in the presence of increasing amounts of uranium imports from other countries. Another factor that needs some consideration in this formulation is the possible effect of the prices of alternate fuels on uranium prices. The price equation (12.4) can be modified to incorporate the effects of meeting the entire uranium demanded from the domestic uranium industry. The cumulative uranium requirements can be calculated as a function of the specified nuclear capacity.

$$q_t^d = f(NCP)_t$$

After the required amounts of uranium for a given level of nuclear capacity have been calculated, the quantity demanded can be set equal to the quantity supplied.

$$q_t^s = q_t^d$$

The uranium price forecasts for an assumed scenario can be derived by rewriting equation 12.1 as follows.

$$\log PU_t = \alpha_0 + \alpha_1 \log RR_t + \alpha_2 \log q_{t-1}^s$$

where q_t^s is an exogenous variable whose value is strictly determined by the level of projected nuclear capacity and by the types of reactors and fuel cycles under consideration. The uranium prices are then expected to be higher than the prices that do not incorporate the condition that all uranium requirements be met from domestic production.

Notes

1. P. Samuelson, *Foundations of Economic Analysis,* Harvard University Press, Cambridge, Mass., 1965; C. Christ, *Econometric Methods,* John Wiley and Sons, New York, 1966.

2. H. Wold, *Econometric Model Building: Notes on the Causal Chain Approach,* North-Holland, Amsterdam, 1964; R.H. Strotz and H. Wold," Recursive vs. Nonrecursive Systems: An Attempt at Synthesis," *Econometrica* 28 (1960):417-427.

3. $F = \dfrac{(e'e - e_1'e_1 - e_2'e)/k}{(e_1'e_1 + e_2'e_2)/(n + m - 2k)}$, $df = k, n + m - 2k$ where $e_1'e$ denotes the sum of square of residuals for the sample period 1959-1975 and $e_2'e_2$ for the sample period 1968-1975. The calculated value of $F_{0.05,5,7}$ is 0.9285, which happens to be less than its critical value 3.97, which suggests the pooling of the two samples.

4. Lewis J. Pearl, "The GESMO Utility Group on U_3O_8 Prices," testimony before the GESMO Hearing Board, U.S. Nuclear Regulatory Commission, April 14, 1977, p. A-2.

13 An Econometric Model

Energy modeling has received much attention during the last few years. A variety of quantitative tools has been used in the formulation of the problem and in the solution of many of the energy issues. Frequently used techniques at the macro as well as at the micro level are input-output, econometrics, system dynamics, and mathematical programming. Econometric modeling has been found best suited for studies of the oil and gas industries in explaining industry behavior, in evaluating implications of policy regulations, and in forecasting prices and outputs.[1]

An Integrated Framework

The present model is recursive in the explanation of industry reserves, output, and prices, and the ordinary least-squares technique is used in the estimation of structural parameters. There are similar microeconometric simulations of other industries.[2] The model is designed to reflect the underlying structure of the physical processes of the uranium-mining industry. The model establishes the relationship between significant individual variables and also the interactions of the relationships among different components of the uranium-mining industry. The model offers the possibility of further improvements and refinements of statistical significance as more data are made available in the future and as the data become more reliable. However, the present model is a comprehensive one, representing the various interrelated aspects of the industry and thereby providing economic credibility to the forecasts of uranium prices.

A flow diagram of the industry, providing a comprehensive view of the major components and their interrelationships, is shown in figure 13-1. The estimation of the structural relationships in different components of the system provided a basis for the model simulation and for the forecasting of uranium prices. The usefulness of the model lies in its ability to predict trends for the desired values of the system. The system's behavior depends on the trends established for the endogenous variables as well as the postulated trends of the exogenous variables that are fed into the system.

The computing recursive scheme for the model simulation is shown in figure 13-2. The initial step in the model simulation is the estimation of total drilling activity TD, which is then used in the determination of cumulative drilling CDR and the number of holes drilled in a given year DND. The informa-

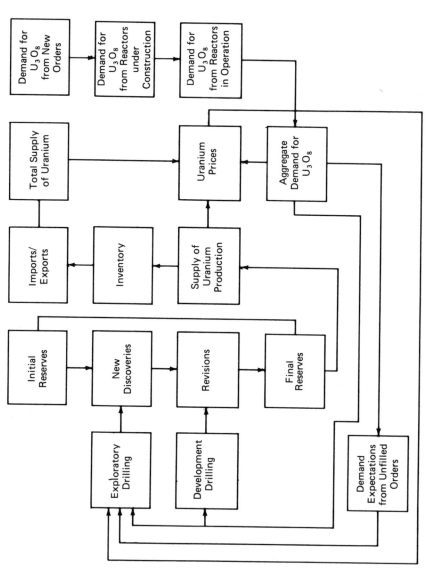

Figure 13-1. System Flow Diagram of Uranium-Mining Industry

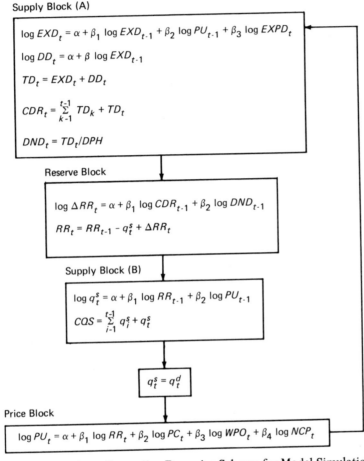

Figure 13-2. Computing Recursive Scheme for Model Simulation

tion obtained in supply block provides a basis for the estimation of addition to reserves ΔRR and of reserves RR in the reserve block of the simulation model. The estimated reserves and the uranium price PU were then used in the calculation of the annual production q^s and of the cumulative quantity of uranium produced in a given year CQS. Finally, the estimated uranium reserves, along with the values of the other variables, determine the price per pound of uranium. The exogenous variables, whose values are forecast, are the cumulative nuclear capacity *NCP*, price of coal *PC*, price of oil *WPO*, and exploratory expenditures *EXPD*.

Different cases were selected for simulation.

Case 1 (Base Case). This case assumes that the nuclear capacity will increase to a level of 380,000 MW by the year 2000. The price of coal is assumed to increase at the rate of 5 percent per year and the price of oil to increase at 6 percent per year. Because of normal increases in nuclear capacity, it is assumed that exploratory expenditures will increase at approximately 6 percent per year.

Case 2 (High-Growth Case). This case assumes that the nuclear capacity will increase at a faster rate, which is made possible by stringent regulatory environmental control and cost increase of coal plants. The nuclear capacity is assumed to reach a level of 620,000 MW. The prices of coal and oil are assumed to increase at the rate of 6 percent and 10 percent respectively. The exploratory expenditures are also assumed to be twice the amount expected in the base case. Such an increase in the exploratory expenditures is felt necessary to take into account the decreasing uranium found per foot drilled.

Case 3 (Low-Growth Case). In this case the nuclear capacity is postulated to increase at a slower rate because of high capital costs for nuclear plants and reduced electric energy consumption. The nuclear capacity is assumed to reach a level of 330,000 MW by the year 2000. Coal and oil prices are allowed to increase by 4 percent per year. The exploratory expenditures are estimated to be a little over half the amount expected for the high-growth case in the year 2000.

Estimation of Parameters

The parameter estimation and the model simulation were done using RAPE, SAS76, and SYSREG programs for regression analysis. The equation numbers shown here for the estimated equations correspond to the earlier formulations in preceding chapters. The estimated equation for the exploratory drilling, with t ratios shown in parentheses, is

$$\log EXD_t = 1.090 + 0.3239 \log EXD_{t-1} + 0.3491 \log PU_{t-1}$$
$$(2.198) \qquad\qquad (0.962)$$

$$+ 0.6166 \log EXPD_t \qquad\qquad (7.1)$$
$$(3.93)$$

$$R^2 = 0.92$$
$$h = 4.59$$

This equation shows a positive sign for the variable exploratory expenditures. This relationship appears reasonable in the evaluation of the effect of exploratory expenditures on the level of exploratory drilling. The t ratio for the price variable is not significant, and further improvement is possible here. The estimated equation for development drilling is

$$\log DD_t = 0.3025 + 0.7843 \log EXD_{t-1}$$
$$(5.64)$$

$$R^2 = 0.5603$$
$$DW = 0.80$$

The low value of Durbin-Watson DW indicates the presence of serial correlation. Since the model developed here is for the purpose of forecasting, the problem of autocorrelation has been corrected. In this case the least-square estimators are not efficient but are unbiased. Furthermore, if residuals have a more complicated structure, second- or higher-order autoregressive, a first-order autoregressive estimation method may give even less efficient estimators than the ordinary least-square method.[3] The equation was then reestimated using the autoregressive procedure. The reestimated equation is

$$\log DD_t = 0.2714 + 0.6806 \log EXD_{t-1}$$
$$(3.68)$$
$$(7.2)$$

$$R^2 = 0.3509$$
$$DW = 1.8$$

The slight change in the values of the coefficient in equation 7.2 indicates that the coefficients are quite stable in the model. The relationship indicates that a 10 percent increase in the exploratory drilling will cause approximately a 7 percent increase in the development drilling effort in the following year. This approximates well the trend observed in the uranium-mining industry.

The equation that describes the relationship between addition to reserves and the other variables is

$$\log \Delta RR_t = 0.804 + 1.21 \log CDR_{t-1} + 0.390 DND_{t-1}$$
$$(2.328) \qquad\qquad (0.799)$$
$$(3.4)$$

$$R^2 = 0.44$$
$$DW = 1.98$$

The sign for the cumulative drilling variable is positive, and the value is greater than unity. In contrast to the gas industry, where cumulative drilling is expected to show a decline in the addition to reserves, uranium discovery shows a positive relationship with drilling effort. This relationship holds true especially in view of the government efforts in providng directions and assistance in the form of the National Uranium Resource Evaluation (NURE) program for the conversion of resources into reserves as more and more drilling is undertaken.

The estimated supply equation is

$$\log q_t^s = -0.0235 + 0.674 \log RR_{t-1} + 0.6602 \log PU_{t-1}$$
$$ (25.24) \qquad\qquad (3.21) \qquad\qquad\qquad (7.7)$$

$$R^2 = 0.9656$$
$$DW = 1.44$$

Finally, the price equation was estimated to be

$$\log PU_t = 8.106 - 0.5321 \log RR_t + 0.00508 \log NCP_t$$
$$ (-2.79) \qquad\qquad (0.370)$$
$$+ 0.03111 \log PC_t + 0.2735 \log WPO_t \qquad\qquad (12.4)$$
$$ (0.163) \qquad\qquad (1.85)$$

$$R^2 = 0.76$$
$$DW = 1.30$$

The coefficients for the variables NCP (nuclear capacity) and WPO (world price of oil) are insignificant in equation 12.4, apparently because of the problem of multicollinearity. For forecasting purposes this problem was not considered serious.

Results of Simulation

The results of the simulation for the three cases are the uranium prices in 1975 dollars (table 13-1). These prices should be considered average prices in a given year. Along with the prices, the cumulative quantities of uranium produced during this period are shown.

The uranium price forecasts shown here will be different from the "spot prices," which reflect the pressures of short-term supply and demand for uranium. These price forecasts are mainly the average uranium delivery prices. Further, these prices do not reflect the possible effects of any state or federal actions on uranium production costs.

The model simulation shows that the prices in all three cases are expected to double during the period 1980–2000. The increases in uranium prices are not going to be sudden and dramatic and are not likely to cause any exponential increase in the cost of electricity generated from nuclear plants.

It is interesting to compare the price forecasts made in this study with those re-

Table 13-1
Forecasts of Uranium Prices and Cumulative Uranium
Production, 1980–2000

Year	Price (1975 Dollars)	Cumulative Uranium Production (Thousands of Tons of U_3O_8)
	Base Case	
1980	25	147.6
1985	32	270.6
1990	36	378.6
1995	42	483.5
2000	47	604.9
	High-Growth Case	
1980	28	147.9
1985	37	273.3
1990	47	385.7
1995	55	502.5
2000	59	686.1
	Low-Growth Case	
1980	23	146.7
1985	28	268.7
1990	33	374.5
1995	36	473.6
2000	40	579.9

ported by the Department of Energy for the years 1980 and 1985. The prices reported by the Department of Energy as of January 1, 1977, reflect the effect of partial purchases of uranium by the nuclear industry for meeting its fuel requirements. The average reported price for delivery in 1980 increased from $11.40 per pound in 1974 to $14.35 per pound of U_3O_8 in 1976 to $18.00 per pound in 1977. As of January 1977 the Department of Energy also reported that the amount of unfilled uranium requirements was of the order of 5,100 tons of uranium for the year 1980 (table 8-2). According to the present study the prices are expected to be within the range of $23 to $28 per pound of U_3O_8 by the year 1980. This increase in prices is likely to result from an upward pressure that will be generated from the unfilled demand for uranium. The price forecasts are compared with the prices reported by the Department of Energy in figure 13-3.

Limitations of the Model

The results of the model should be interpreted carefully for the following reasons.

1. Uncertainty has been a common phenomenon in the uranium markets.

Nuclear Fuel and Energy Policy

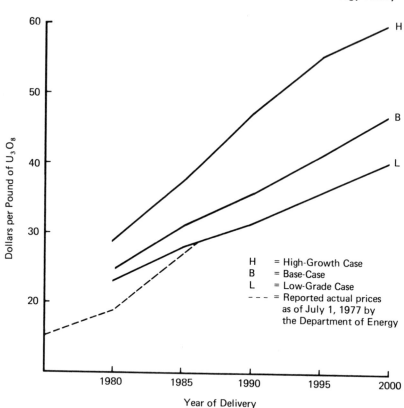

Figure 13-3. Forecasts of Average Uranium Prices and Actual Prices Reported by the Department of Energy

The forecasts are made on the assumption of continuity of certain postulated trends in the uranium-mining industry as well as in the nuclear industry. The present analysis does not incorporate the effect of uncertainty on the future supplies, demand, and prices of uranium.

2. The results of the model are as good as the data fed into the system for simulation. The reliability of the data has been an extremely important factor in the present analysis. Further improvements are possible as more reliable and adequate information becomes available in the future.

3. The uranium data on reserves have not been adjusted for inflationary effects. This may have introduced some bias in the analysis and forecasts of uranium prices.

4. At present the international trade has no influence on the production and prices of uranium in domestic markets. In the future the domestic ura-

nium prices and production should be tied to the developments in the international uranium mining and milling industry.

5. The present study assumes that the competitive environment prevails in the uranium markets. This assumption should be tested empirically, and the implications for forecasting future uranium prices and outputs should be studied.

6. The results of the price and output forecasts in the development of policies concerning the future nuclear programs should be evaluated along with other major environmental impacts as well as social impacts and governmental regulations.

Notes

1. M. Kennedy, "An Econometric Model of the World Oil Market," *Bell J. Econ. Man. Sci.* 5 (1974):540-577; P. Rice, "An Econometric Model of the U.S. Petroleum Industry," Ph.D. Thesis, State University of New York, Stony Brook, 1976; P.W. MacAvoy and R.S. Pindyck, "Alternative Regulatory Policies for Dealing with the Natural Gas Shortages," *Bell J. Econ. Man. Sci.* (1973): 454-498; J.D. Khazzoom, "The FPC Staffs' Econometric Model of Natural Gas Supply in the United States," *Bell J. Econ. Man. Sci.* (1971):51-93; E. Erickson and R. Spann, "Supply Response in a Regulated Industry: The Case of Natural Gas," *Bell J. Econ. Man. Sci.* 2 (1971):94-121.

2. J.M. Vernon et al., "An Econometric Model of the Tobacco Industry," *Rev. Econ. Stat.* 51 (1969):149-158; W.H. Wallace et al., "An Econometric Model of the Textile Industry in the United States," *Rev. Econ. Stat.* 50 (1968):13-22; F.M. Fisher et al., "An Econometric Model of the World Copper Industry," *Bell J. Econ. Man. Sci.* 3 (1972):568-609; J.M. Griffin, "The Effects of Higher Prices on Electricity Consumption," *Bell J. Econ. Man. Sci.* 5 (1974):515-539.

3. R.F. Engle, "Specification of the Disturbance for Efficient Estimation," *Econometrica,* 42 (1974):135-146.

14 Characteristics of the Enrichment Industry

The Department of Energy owns and operates three enrichment plants located in Oak Ridge, Tennessee, Paducah, Kentucky, and Portsmouth, Ohio. In recent years changes in the ownership of the enrichment operations have been proposed. Uranium Enrichment Associates, a private industry consortium, proposed to build an enrichment plant with sufficient guarantees from the federal government. The Nuclear Fuel Assurance Act, which was designed to give the initial support and liability for private industry operations, failed to pass in Congress. This measure made it difficult for private enterprise, especially the smaller organizations, to enter the uranium enrichment market. Currently Exxon is pursuing research in enrichment technology and may become a potential supplier of enriched fuel in the private sector.

Industry Structure

The uranium enrichment industry is different from the other industries in the nuclear fuel cycle operations in several of its economic characteristics. The reason for the distinct pattern of the uranium enrichment industry is due mainly to the nature and the purpose for which this product was produced and consumed at an early stage of the noncommercial nuclear phase. The industry constituted a single producer and a single buyer of this product. Further, the federal government was the sole producer as well as the sole consumer of the enriched fuel. Since uranium was enriched for military purposes before the era of the nuclear electric industry, the product never entered the phase of commercial transactions in the uranium market.

The entry of the nuclear industry in the early 1960s as a competitive source of electric power brought several changes in the structure of the uranium enrichment industry. Though the federal government has remained the only supplier of this product, the number of buyers for this product increased in proportion to the growth of power plants in the nuclear industry. In the uranium enrichment market the buyers included domestic as well as foreign electric utilities. The federal government has continued to be the buyer, in lesser quantities, of enriched fuel for defense purposes.

The degree of monopoly control by the U.S. government in the production and pricing of enriched fuel is likely to be lessened when the proposed new enrichment plants are built in Europe. The development of enrichment programs in Europe will to some extent provide a competitive basis for the efficient control of production costs in domestic enrichment plants. The uranium enrichment industry can currently be described as a monopoly on the producer's side, as the consumers have little if any influence on the production and pricing policies of uranium enrichment.

Enrichment Pricing

The economic basis for any pricing policy is governed mainly by the concept of the efficiency of resource allocation. In a competitive enterprise system the product prices reflect the alternative costs of providing additional amounts of various goods and services. The efficiency concept requires that the price be determined at a point where the demand intersects the marginal cost curve. However, the principle of "marginal cost pricing" does not have any relevance to public utilities, which are regulated monopolies. The rates of such monopolies are regulated for allowing the cost recovery either on a "historical or original costs" basis or on the basis of average cost of service provided to the customer. An economic comparison of federally owned uranium enrichment operations with a single commercial firm operating in a competitive environment is not realistic or meaningful. Further, it is doubtful whether private industry can enter the enrichment market as a main competitor with the Energy Research and Development Administration's enrichment operations during this century. However, it may be possible for ERDA to transfer some of its enrichment contracts to the private sector whenever a private company such as Exxon can offer the service. Since it tends to be a monopoly, the enrichment industry is more like an electric utility than any other firm operating in the private sector of the U.S. economy.

At the same time the enrichment industry cannot be classified as a regulated monopoly, since only congress directly regulates its activities. Congress from time to time determines the fair price to be charged to electric utilities.

Description of Enrichment Operation

Uranium concentrate supplied by a customer to the enrichment plants contains 0.71 percent of U-235 and about 99.3 percent of U-238. The U-235 is a fissionable material and should be enriched to about 3 percent for use as a fuel in the nuclear reactors. In the enrichment process a certain amount of U-235 is left in the tails. The effort required in uranium enrichment depends on the enrichment tails.

The separative work unit is a measure of the amount of physical effort required to separate the isotopes of uranium. The amount of effort required

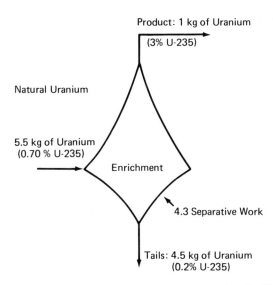

Figure 14-1. Relationship between Natural Uranium Feed, Tails, and Final Enriched Fuel

in the separation of isotopes depends on the quantities and assay of the three streams—feed, product, and the tails, as shown in figure 14-1. ERDA receives the customer's uranium feed in the form of uranium hexafluoride (UF_6), which is the gaseous form of uranium. For example, a customer will provide 5.5 kilograms of natural uranium and receives 1 kilogram of uranium that is 3 percent U-235 enriched. These operations leave 4.5 kilograms of tails containing 0.2 percent of U-235. The tails assay refers to the amount of U-235 that remains in the tail streams of an enrichment plant. Performing this separation work takes 4.3 separative work units. The amount of natural uranium and the separative work units to recover 1 kilogram of 3 percent U-235 enriched uranium vary as a function of percent of tails assay requirements.

| | *Tails Assay (percent)* | | |
	0.20	*0.25*	*0.30*
Natural uranium (kilograms)	5.5	6.0	6.6
Separative work units (SWU)	4.3	3.8	3.4

The tails assay determines the amount of feed and separative work required to obtain 1 kilogram of enriched uranium. As the tails assay increases from 0.2 percent to 0.3 percent, the total natural uranium required to produce 1 kilogram of enriched fuel increases from 5.5 kilograms to 6.6 kilograms. This measure, however, will decrease the separative work requirements from 4.3 SWU to 3.4 SWU. The optimum tails assay is generally determined on the basis of either minimizing the electric power consumption or of extending the supplies of natural uranium.

Two types of tails assay are generally referred to in enrichment operations: operating tails assay and transaction tails assay. The operating tails assay refers to the actual concentration of U-235 left in the waste generated by a uranium enrichment plant. The operating tails assay was set at 0.2 at the beginning of ERDA's operations to provide commercial enrichment services to utility. Beginning July 1, 1971, the operating tails were increased to 0.3 percent of U-235, since the government wanted to deplete its excess natural stock by using it as feed to the gaseous diffusion plants. Further the separative work requirements are about 20 percent less if the decision is to operate at 0.3 percent rather than at 0.2 percent, and this difference will increase the uranium ore requirements to about 26 percent more in quantity.[1] From July 1, 1975, to the present the operating tails assay has been set at 0.25 percent of U-235.

The transaction tails assay determined the agreement that a customer enters into with ERDA concerning the amount of enrichment services to be purchased. This agreement determines the amount of uranium feed that will be delivered by a customer to the enrichment plant in return for a certain amount of enriched uranium. The transaction tails have been set at 0.2 percent of U-235 from the beginning of ERDA's enriching services in 1960s.

Note

1. Mitre Corporation, *Nuclear Power Issues and Choices,* Ballinger, Cambridge, Mass., 1976, p. 368; Energy Research and Development Administration, *Uranium Enrichment Conference,* Conf-751134, Oak Ridge, Tennessee, November 11, 1975.

15 Demand for and Supply of Enrichment

There are a few operating plants in the world that have sizable uranium enrichment capacity. These plants are being operated in the United States, the Soviet Union, France, and the United Kingdom. The United States is currently the world's leading supplier of uranium enrichment services. The future trends in the world nuclear generating capacity will be an important factor in determining the total demand for the U.S. enrichment capacity. The future enrichment programs of foreign countries will also have some influence on the expansion of U.S. enrichment capacity. Some of the important factors governing the demand for and supply of enrichment services are briefly analyzed.

Demand for Enrichment

The following factors have some bearing on the future enrichment demand:

Domestic and foreign nuclear capacity

Domestic and foreign nuclear reactor mix

Recycling and reprocessing of U and PU (domestic and abroad)

Enrichment tails assay

Government requirements

Stockpile quantities

Other factors also have some effects on the demand for uranium enrichment. These are the fuel cycle lead times, thermal efficiencies, irradiation level, and nuclear plant capacity factors. The reactor mix of the world nuclear generating capacity will consist primarily of the lightwater reactors during the period 1977–2000. A 1,000-MW lightwater reactor requires approximately 100,000 SWU per year to meet its fuel needs.[1]

Another factor that will have an effect on the demand for enrichment is the policy concerning recycling and reprocessing of uranium and plutonium. Fears concerning theft of nuclear material by terrorists and proliferation of nuclear weapons have closed this option temporarily in the nuclear fuel cycle of the U.S. nuclear industry. The reprocessing of spent fuel is allowed for the pur-

Table 15-1

United States Enrichment Demand for "Low" and "Conservation" Cases at Varying Tails Assay, 1976-2000

(in millions of SWU)

	Tails Assay							
	0.20%		0.25%		0.275%		0.30%	
Year	Low	Cons.	Low	Cons.	Low	Cons.	Low	Cons.
1976	5.8	5.8	5.1	5.1	4.8	4.8	4.6	4.6
1980	9.1	9.1	8.1	8.1	7.6	7.6	7.2	7.2
1985	16.5	15.6	14.6	13.8	13.8	13.1	13.1	12.4
1990	24.7	22.3	21.9	19.7	20.7	18.7	19.6	17.7
1995	34.3	29.7	30.4	26.2	28.7	24.8	27.3	23.6
2000	43.7	38.1	38.7	33.7	36.6	31.9	43.7	30.3

Source: Energy Research and Development Administration, Energy Systems Analysis Branch, Office of Planning and Analysis, "Forecast of Nuclear Capacity, Separative Work, Uranium, and Related Quantities: U.S. Low Case and Conservation Case, No. FBR—No Repro—70 percent CF," August and October 1976.

pose of plutonium recovery for use as mixed oxide fuel. This action will cause a considerable reduction in the demand for enrichment.

The U.S. government's annual requirements are estimated to be around 1.7 million SWU. In the past the policy concerning the stockpile quantities, which serve the purpose of in-process and buffer inventories, has been to carry the stock equivalent to one hundred days of annual SWU capacity. In addition, a certain amount of SWU is carried for contingencies.

The U.S. enrichment demand for separative work units for the nuclear capacity forecasts in the low and conservation scenarios, which were used earlier in model simulation as base case and low-growth case, are shown in table 15-1 for varying tails assay. The reduction in SWU demand in the conservation case compared with the low case becomes noticeable after 1985. Since the most likely tails assays are considered to be 0.20 percent and 0.25 percent, the domestic demand for SWU by the year 2000 is estimated to be in the range of 34 million to 44 million SWU.

Supply of Enrichment Services

Alternative technologies are being developed for enrichment in different parts of the world. Gaseous diffusion is currently the predominant technology in the enrichment industry and has proven to be a feasible alternative for large-scale enrichment operations.

The gaseous diffusion process operates on the principle of mass differences and the thermal energy of the uranium hexafluoride molecule UF_6.[2] The molecules containing U-235 weigh less than U-238 molecules and travel at a faster speed. In the gaseous diffusion process a wall with numerous holes is erected. When the gas UF_6 is passed through a cascade with several hundreds of barriers erected, it becomes enriched in U-235 isotope.

The gas centrifuge method uses the differences in the density of the two isotopes of uranium to separate them. When the UF_6 is placed in a spinning centrifuge, the heavier and denser U-238 is diffused to the outside wall while the U-235 remains at the center. The feed is sent through the cascade until the desired quantity of enriched uranium is derived.

The separation nozzle utilizes the principle of the molecules containing U-235 which weigh less than the molecules of U-238. In this process the UF_6 is forced out of a nozzle at a very high speed and hits the curved wall. At the end of the curved wall a knife blade divides the flow into enriched UF_6 and the tails. The gas then cascades until the desired level of enrichment is reached. Another process that is similar to the use of the separation nozzle is the stationary wall centrifuge, which has the similar separation technology.

Laser isotope separation (LIS) has two techniques that are similar in many ways. In the atomic method elemental uranium is exposed to a laser very carefully tuned to a wavelength of light or an ultraviolet in which the U-235 will be absorbed, leaving the U-238. With this power the U-235 will be at an excited level. A less powerful laser is used to ionize the U-235, causing the U-235 to take on a plus atomic charge. The U-235 atoms are then collected by using a negatively charged plate. The other method, known as the molecular method, is similar to the atomic method except that a lower-powered laser is required and the gas is cooled by an expanding nozzle technique.

There are a number of aerodynamic processes; some of the variations to this technique are the separation tube, the separation probe, massed beam, velocity slips, and the jet membrane. As an example, the jet membrane is a stream of UF_6 colliding with a fast-moving expanding jet of condensable gas. The light molecules of U-235 penetrate the jet more easily. In this case a tube collects the enriched gas, while the depleted one is left as a condensed gas.

Another method of enrichment is to apply the plasma technique. Plasma is rotated much faster than in a centrifuge using a changing magnetic field. This technique results in a large separation factor and can enrich uranium. Another method of separation is to place plasma of UF_6 or elemental uranium in a strong uniform magnetic field. It is then exposed to a low-energy radio frequency wave that is resonant with the cyclotron frequency of the U-235 ions. This rotation then makes the separation of U-235 possible. Another technique involves the enrichment of UF_6 plasma by chemi-ionization. In this method the UF_6 gas is accelerated to supersonic speeds by an expanding jet of inert gas. The gas is then ionized by a cross beam of sodium.

Table 15-2

An Economic Comparison of Alternative Processes Relative to Gaseous Diffusion

	Specific Capital Investment	Power Cost	Operating Costs Other than Power
Centrifuge	>	<	>
Separation nozzle[a]	<	>	≅
Stationary-walled centrifuge[a]	≅	≅	?
LIS-atomic	<	<	>
LIS-molecular	<	<	>
Chemical exchange: U^{IV} (aq)-U^{VI} (org)	≅	<	>
Other Aerodynamic Processes	>	>	≅
Plasma: Chemi-ionization	>	<	>

Source: P.R. Vanstrum and S.A. Levin, "New Processes for Uranium Isotope Separation," International Atomic Energy Agency–CN–36, Union Carbide Corporation, May 1977.

Note: ≅, Approximately equal to the diffusion process; >, < greater than or less than the diffusion process respectively;? unknown.

[a]Based on estimates made by the process developers.

An economic comparison of alternative technologies is provided in table 15-2. The capital costs, power costs, and the operating and maintenance costs of different processes are compared with the diffusion process. The centrifuge, aerodynamic processes, and plasma:chemi-ionization processes are relatively capital intensive enrichment technologies. With the exception of the separation nozzle and aerodynamic processes, all the new enrichment technologies require less electric power than the gaseous diffusion method. The new technologies seem to offer a definite potential for reducing the cost of electric power in the effort required to separate isotopes. Another interesting feature of these new technologies is that most require higher operating costs than the known gaseous diffusion technology. No definite cost comparison can be made with these new technologies because most of them are still in the experimental stage.

U.S. Enrichment Capacity

The present existing capacity of the three ERDA plants is estimated to be around 17 million SWU, if fully powered. The maximum enrichment capacity is not currently being utilized because of the lack of required electric power supply to enrichment plants. But by the year 1985 the situation is assumed to be different, and the maximum capacity is expected to be fully powered. The plans to improve the operations of the existing plants through cascade improvement

Table 15-3
United States Enrichment Supply: Existing, Planned, and Additional
Supply, 1975-2000
(in millions of SWU)

Year	Existing Supply	Supply from Improvements	Additional Supply from Centrifuge	Total
1975	13.3	–	–	13.3
1980	16.8	7.8	–	24.6
1985	17.2	10.5	–	27.7
1990	17.2	10.5	8.8	36.7
1995	17.2	10.5	9.0+	?
2000	17.2	10.5	9.0+	?

Source: Department of Energy, Planning Division, *Uranium Enrichment*, Oak Ridge, Tennessee, June 1977.

(CIP) and cascade upgrading (CUP) programs will add an additional capacity of approximately 11 million SWU by 1985. According to the national energy plan there will be an additional capacity of 9 million SWU utilizing the gas centrifuge process which will be constructed at Portsmouth, Ohio.

The total U.S. enrichment capacity for the period 1975-2000 is shown in table 15-3. The present schedule indicates that the total enrichment capacity can meet demand for SWU up to the year 1990. Beyond the year 1990 enrichment capacity must be increased. Much progress has been made in the basic research, experimental operation, and development of advanced models for centrifuge technology. An accumulation of about 5 million hours of machine operations on UF_6 points out that centrifuge technology is highly competitive with diffusion and can be in operation in the middle to later 1980s.[3]

Currently ERDA has long-term contracts to supply the fuel needs of 361 reactors which have the total generating capacity of 323 GW of nuclear power. This includes 118 GW of foreign nuclear capacity.

World Enrichment Capacity

The enrichment plants in operation, other than the ones in the United States, are in the Soviet Union, France, and the United Kingdom. The Soviet plants are said to be mainly of gaseous diffusion and estimated to have the capacity of about 7 million to 8 million SWU per year, about half of which is believed to be in operation (table 15-4). Eurodiff and Coredif are multinational organizations having the same members, Belgium, France, Iran, Italy, and Spain. However, the arrangement of shareholding by these countries is different in these two orga-

Table 15-4
World Enrichment Capacity, 1977–1990
(in millions of SWU)

Year	Firm and Likely							Including Potential Additional Capacity				Total Firm, Lively, and Potential
	ERDA	ERDA Add-on	Eurodif	Coredif	Urenco	USSR	Total Firm and Likely	Brazil	Japan	South Africa	Total Potential	
1977	18.0				0.2	0.7	18.9					
1978	20.3				0.4	1.5	22.2					
1979	22.2		2.6		0.8	2.0	27.6					
1980	24.6		6.1		0.9	2.7	34.3					
1981	25.5		8.4		1.4	2.6	37.9					
1982	25.6		10.8		2.0	2.6	41.0	0.1	0.1		0.2	41.2
1983	26.6		10.8		2.0	3.0	41.4	0.1	0.1		0.2	41.6
1984	26.6		10.8	2.0	4.0	4.0	47.4	0.2	0.2	0.5	0.9	48.3
1985	28.0		10.8	4.5	5.5	4.0	52.8	0.2	0.2	2.0	2.4	55.2
1986	28.0	0.6	10.8	5.0	7.0	4.0	55.4	0.8	0.8	3.5	5.1	60.5
1987	28.0	3.3	10.8	8.0	8.5	4.0	62.6	0.8	0.8	5.0	6.6	69.2
1988	28.0	6.6	10.8	9.0	10.0	4.0	68.4	1.0	1.0	6.5	8.5	76.9
1989	28.0	8.8	10.8	9.0	10.0	4.0	70.6	1.0	1.0	8.0	10.0	80.6
1990	28.0	8.8	10.8	9.0	10.0	4.0	70.6	2.0	1.0	8.0	11.0	81.6

Source: Department of Energy, Planning Division, *Uranium Enrichment*, Oak Ridge, Tennessee, June 1977.

nizations. Eurodiff plans to build a gaseous diffusion plant of the size 10.8 million SWU at Pierrelatte in the south of France by the year 1982. Eurodiff is expected to have 2.6 million SWU of capacity in operation in the year 1979, France is also sponsoring Coredif to bring a second diffusion plant of 9 million SWU per year, and 4.5 million SWU of capacity is likely to be completed in 1985. Urenco is another multinational organization, whose members are Great Britain, the Netherlands, and West Germany. Urenco has plans for 5.5 million SWU of capacity by 1985 and 10 million SWU of capacity by 1990. Brazil, Japan, and South Africa have conditional plans for developing enrichment capacity. Brazil is likely to have a small capacity of 0.2 million SWU by 1985, and it is expected to reach 2.0 million SWU by 1990. Japan has been actively seeking partnership with other countries who can provide uranium feed and enrichment technology. Japan plans to have 1 million SWU capacity by 1990. South Africa's enrichment plants, with a capacity of 0.5 million, SWU, will be in operation in 1984, and this may increase to 8 million SWU by 1990.

The world enrichment capacity, including potential additional, is likely to be well above 150 million SWU by 1990. The present trends in the world nuclear generating capacity, in the demand and supply of separative work, indicate an excess of enrichment capacity until 1990 without plutonium recycling. At least in the immediate future there is no fear of any real shortages in the world supply of enrichment capacity.[4]

Notes

1. D.C. Thomas, "Uranium Cartel: Domestic Impact," hearings before the Subcommittee on Oversight and Investigations of the Committee on Interstate and Foreign Commerce, U.S. House of Representatives, August 15, 1977, p. 2; for an assessment of world's demand for and the supply of enrichment services, see, J.J. Steyn, "Assessment of Domestic and Foreign Separative Work Supply and Demand," paper presented at the American Nuclear Society Executive Conference on Uranium Fuel Supply, Monterey, California, January 23–26, 1977.

2. Matt Hoyt of the University of Tennessee assisted in describing the alternative enrichment technologies.

3. E.B. Kiser, *Review of U.S. Gas Centrifuge Program*, paper presented at the Atomic Industrial Forum, Fuel Cycle Conference, 1977.

4. For a detailed discussion and analysis of nuclear fuel cycle requirements for the world nuclear industry, see, Organization for Economic Cooperation and Development, *Nuclear Fuel Cycle Requirements and Supply Considerations through the Long Term*, Paris, 1978.

16 Fuel Enrichment Costs

The method adopted by the Energy Research and Development Administration (ERDA) in the calculation of the cost of separative work is different, in some respects, from the practices commonly used in a business firm. The main differences lie in the taxes and the return on capital which are not shown in the preparation of the costs of ERDA. According to the Atomic Energy Act of 1954, the government charge for separative work was to cover its costs of operations distributed over a campaign period. The three ERDA plants were built earlier for defense purposes and were being amortized under military programs. There is, however, still some depreciation left to be recovered from plant and equipment and from the capital improvements.

Ceiling Charge

There have been several attempts to formulate an equitable pricing system. One of these measures was the ceiling charge. A ceiling charge formula was developed so that ERDA would not charge its customers more than the ceiling price for the requirement type of contract executed before May 9, 1973. The ceiling charge is computed on the basis of a $30 historical charge escalated by the prices of the inputs power and labor and weighted in the ratio of 15 to 5 with a fixed-cost component of $10. The base rates for power and labor were set equal to 3.958 mills/kWh and $2.78/hr respectively. The ceiling charge was then calculated:[1]

$$CC = \$10 + \$15(P/3.958) + \$5(L/2.87)$$

where

CC = ceiling charge in dollars

P = the cost of power in mills/kwh to enrichment plants

L = current value of the wage rate for the chemicals and allied products industry

The costs of power and labor along with the escalation rates of these cost components for ceiling charge for the period 1966–1977 are shown in table 16-1.

Table 16–1

Price Escalation and Cost Components of Ceiling Charge, 1966–1977

Year	Power Costs *Power Costs*	*Power Rate (mills/kwh)*	*Power Escalation*	*Labor Costs* Labor Costs	*Labor Rate (dollars/hr)*	*Labor Escalation*	*All Other*	Ceiling Charge ($/SWU)
1966	$15.00			$ 5.00			$10	$30.00
1967	15.05	3.97	$ 0.05	5.12	$2.94	$0.12	10	30.17
1968	15.39	4.06	0.39	5.31	3.05	0.31	10	30.70
1969	15.45	4.07	0.45	5.59	3.21	0.59	10	31.04
1970	15.77	4.16	0.77	5.92	3.40	0.92	10	31.69
1971	16.60	4.38	1.60	6.31	3.62	1.31	10	32.91
1972	19.98	5.27	4.98	6.74	3.87	1.74	10	36.72
1973	21.23	5.60	6.23	7.21	4.14	2.21	10	38.44
1974	24.37	6.05	7.94	7.74	4.39	2.65	10	40.59
1975	29.10	7.67	14.10	8.17	4.69	3.17	10	47.27
1976	40.71	10.74	25.71	9.07	5.22	4.09	10	59.80
1977[a]	$45.83	12.09	$30.83	$10.00	$5.74	$5.00	$10	$65.83

Source: Calculated from A.J. Rossi and F.A. Ritchings, "Dramatic Changes in Nuclear and Fuel Costs," Paper presented at the 47th Executive Conference, Hilton Head Island, South Carolina, Ebasco Services, Inc., October 1976, p. 9.
[a]Estimate

The increase in the power costs to enrichment plants was minimal until 1971; then these costs showed small increases until 1974. The oil embargo in 1973 almost doubled power costs in a period of three years, 1974–1977, whereas the increases in labor costs, which were added to the base costs, showed a more modest increase. The ceiling charge will continue to constrain the maximum prices that ERDA can charge on its requirements contract.

Base Unit Costs

In estimating the cost of the separative work unit, the Department of Energy first develops a long-term operational plan. In a given period of time the supply of separative work and the separative work costs depend on the operating plans developed by ERDA. The operating plan is designed primarily with the objective of meeting the demand for separative work units by the electric utilities. The cost minimization criterion enters the operating plans as long as it can satisfy the constraint of meeting the demand for SWU. The cost recovery charge as determined by the Department of Energy is described as a two-step process. At the first stage the operating plan is developed. At the second stage the costs associated with such a plan are estimated and levelized over a pricing campaign period. The development of an operating plan provides a basis for the calculation of base unit cost for uranium enrichment. The base unit cost is calculated as follows.

$$BUC = \frac{\Sigma[PV \text{ costs} - PV \text{ revenues}]}{\Sigma PV \text{ } SWU}$$

$$= \frac{\Sigma(1 + i)^{-k} (C_k - R_k)}{\Sigma(1 + i)^{-k} D_k + (1 + i)^{-n} I_n}$$

where

BUC = base unit cost in dollars per SWU

$(1 + i)^{-k}$ = discount factor

PV = present value

C_k = total costs, which include out-of-pocket costs, nonfund costs, and imputed interest in enrichment activity assets at time k

R_k = revenues from SWU sales

D_k = demand for enriched uranium

I_n = ending inventory

The base unit cost is then increased by a factor of 1.15, representing 15 percent increase in the costs per SWU to provide for contingencies and unforeseen escalation in factor prices.

The first basic unit charge was $26 during the period 1968–1970 and was increased to $28.70 in 1972. The increase was made on the basis of the average power cost rate of 4.5 mills/kwh. This charge was further increased to $32.00 on the basis of 5.2 mills per kilowatt-hour of power costs. The cost of electric power supplied to ERDA by different electric producing agencies for the years 1970 and 1972 is shown in table 16–2.

The cost per separative work unit continued to increase. In 1974 the Atomic Energy Commission (AEC) further raised the charge, to $47.80 per SWU for requirement contracts and to $42.10 per SWU for fixed-commitment contracts follows. The $8.24 increase in cost per SWU was broken down as follows:[2]

1. Power costs, $4.17
2. Changes in nonpower GDP costs, forecast demand, provisional operating plan and $U_3 O_8$ market prices, $0.93
3. Centrifuge research and development, $2.42
4. Increase in the government cost of money from 5.5 percent to 6 percent, $0.72

Table 16-2

Cost of Electric Power Supplied to ERDA Enrichment Plants in 1970
and 1972

(mills per kwh)

Plant	1970	1972
TVA		
Oak Ridge	4.53	5.55
Paducah	4.22	5.53
EEI		
Paducah	4.59	5.37
OVEC		
Portsmouth	4.05	4.55
Weighted Average	4.32	5.20

Source: Uranium Enrichment Pricing Criteria, Hearings before the Joint Committee on Atomic Energy, 92nd Congress, February 25, 1971, part 2, p. 40.

In June 1975 ERDA announced the price increase to $53.35 per SWU to customers holding fixed-commitment contracts and to $60.95 per SWU to requirement contract customers. The base unit price for SWU in 1977 was $64.70.

A detailed breakdown of the cost per SWU calculated for the year 1977 is shown in table 16-3. A risk charge of $5.10 is added to the cost of $64.64, to determine the requirement type contract charge of $69.80 per separative work unit. This charge was still limited by ceiling charge. And by proper accounting of credit payments of $3.40, the fixed-commitment charge was estimated at $61.30.

Table 16-3

Cost Breakdown per SWU (Requirements Type and Fixed Commitment)
(in 1977 dollars)

Cost Component	Dollars per SWU	Percentage
Power	29.50	45.6
Other diffusion operating	4.81	7.5
Diffusion capital projects	4.25	6.6
Centrifuge and working capital	2.47	3.8
Base plant and working capital	5.50	8.5
Split tails feed	2.74	4.3
Interest on preproduction	6.94	10.7
Contingency (15%)	8.43	13.0
Total	64.64	100.0

Source: Department of Energy, Planning Division, *Uranium Enrichment,* Oak Ridge, Tennessee, June 1977.

Future Enrichment Costs

At the end of June 1976 ERDA submitted a draft to Congress asking that the Atomic Energy Act of 1954 be amended to allow ERDA to revise the basis for establishing the fair price for enrichment services. This amendment was intended to provide a basis for fair value where the enrichment costs were not to be less than its production costs over a reasonable period of time. This cost would include factors such as taxes and insurance that had not been included before in the determination of price per SWU.

The earlier decision to build the gaseous diffusion plant has been revised, and instead a centrifuge plant is being constructed at Portsmouth, Ohio. An attractive feature of centrifuge technology is that it requires only about 4 percent of the electric power consumed in a diffusion plant to provide the same level of service. This aspect of centrifuge is important given the future uncertainty of electric power costs and the reliability of power supply to enrichment plants.

The unit cost of separative work for a gas centrifuge plant is expected to be much lower than the unit cost for a gaseous diffusion plant built at a given site. A reasonable price for fuel enrichment from a newly built gas centrifuge plant is estimated to be approximately $100 per SWU. However, the unit cost depends on the capital charge used in the calculations.[3] This price according to the present analysis is judged to be a fair price.

The rate at which the future uranium prices will be escalated from the present level of $100 per SWU depends on several factors, both internal and external to the enrichment industry. A comprehensive view of the enrichment operations that have direct and indirect effects on the cost of enrichment is shown in figure 16–1. Feasible paths, each representing a set of factors, are portrayed in the diagram leading to final demand for SWU. The sequence in which these factors are arranged is unimportant, because they are independent of each other. A host of economic, environmental, technological, and institutional factors reduces the number of alternative routes to a few routes in the short-term analysis of the demand for and supply of enrichment. A significant decrease in the future enrichment cost may come from the commercial applications of laser isotope separation technology. Similarly a dramatic increase in power costs to ERDA plants may cause a substantial increase in the enrichment costs. The chances of a successful realization of laser enrichment and multifold increases in the cost of electric power during this century are very small. The future enrichment costs may be escalated, from a base of 1977 price, at a rate commensurate with the general inflationary rate in the U.S. economy.

The uncertainty that surrounded the growth of nuclear power had an impact on the planning and development of the uranium enrichment industry. Existing and planned enrichment capacity can meet the enrichment needs of nuclear reactors up to 1990. Beyond 1990 additional capacity must come on-line at ERDA plants.

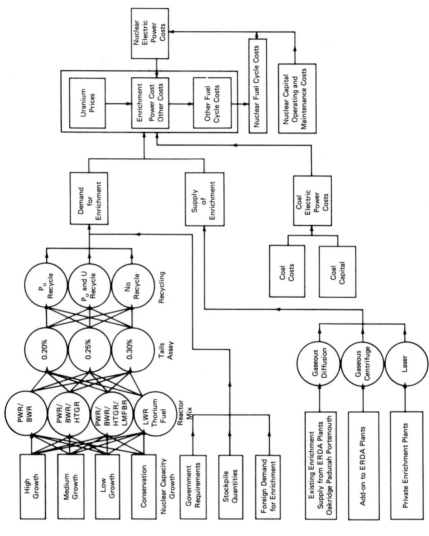

Figure 16-1. Flow Diagram of Demand for and Supply of Uranium Enrichment Services

Notes

1. Uranium Enrichment Pricing Criteria, hearings before the Joint Committee on Atomic Energy, 92nd Congress, February 25, 1971, part 2, p. 40.

2. Future Structure of the Uranium Enrichment Industry, hearings before the Joint Committee on Atomic Energy, 93rd Congress, part 3, vol. 1, 1974, p. 79.

3. Department of Energy, Planning Division, *Uranium Enrichment,* Oak Ridge, Tennessee, June 1977.

17 Nuclear Fuel Costs

The nuclear fuel costs include the costs of uranium mining and milling, conversion to uranium hexafluoride, uranium enrichment, fabrication of fuel elements, spent fuel storage, waste management, and transportation of fuel. The fuel costs are generally classified as front-end costs and back-end costs of the fuel cycle. The costs incurred prior to the irradiation of the life cycle of the nuclear fuel are the front-end costs. So far the costs of uranium mining and milling and the costs of uranium enrichment have been examined. The analysis of the costs of UF_6 conversion and fuel fabrication complete the analysis of front-end costs.

The back-end costs comprise the costs of spent fuel storage, waste management, and the transportation of fuel. The plant decommissioning costs are also a part of the back-end costs of the nuclear fuel cycle. The back-end costs are less adaptable to economic analysis because they are influenced, to a great extent, by government regulations. These costs require a careful and thorough analysis within a socioeconomic framework incorporating national and international policies. The uncertainty that surrounds future developments in government policies affecting the recycling of nuclear waste makes it much more difficult, at this time, to provide any indications of future trends in the back-end costs of the fuel cycle. At the present these costs are assumed to remain constant for the next twenty-five years.[1]

UF_6 Conversion Costs

After mining and milling of uranium ore the product is concentrated in the form of yellowcake. The ore concentrate is then converted into uranium hexafluoride, UF_6, which is suitable for enrichment in gaseous diffusion plants. Two methods are available for the production of uranium hexafluoride. One method is the dry hydrofluor process, in which the concentrate passes through several stages of operation, including reduction, hydrofluorination, fluorination, and distillation. The product is finally delivered as UF_6 to enrichment plants. The other method is called the wet solvent extraction process where the wet solvent extraction occurs before reduction, hydrofluorination, and fluorination.[2]

The production technology for UF_6 is relatively simple and requires smaller amounts of capital inputs than other stages of operations in the nuclear fuel cycle. The estimated time required for building a 5,000-ton commercial uranium plant is two years.[3] The development and expansion of the UF_6 production activity depends on expectations concerning the future demand for uranium. The simplistic nature of the conversion operations makes the cost projections much easier than other facets of nuclear fuel production. Currently there are six commercial plants in operation in the United States, France, United Kingdom, and Canada: two in the United States, two in France, one in Canada, and one in the United Kingdom. In the United States Allied Chemical and Kerr-McGee have a total operating capacity of 19,000 tons a year.[4]

Few studies have estimated the future costs of conversion. A study at the Oak Ridge National Laboratory suggests that future trends in the costs of conversion of UF_6 be related to possible changes in the Composite Price Index.[5] The Composite Price Index is derived by assigning relative weights to the average hourly wage, the wholesale price index, and to a fixed component of the conversion price. This study estimates that the conversion costs will be \$4.27 and \$4.55 per kilogram of uranium in 1980 and 1985 respectively. A similar study by EBASCO Services Inc. forecasts that conversion costs will be \$5.40, \$5.85, and \$8.65 per kilogram of uranium for 1986, 1988, and 1998 respectively.[6] The assumption underlying these forecasts is that future costs are expected to increase at the rate of 4 percent to 5 percent per year, which is consistent with the expected general inflationary rate in the economy. The Nuclear Regulatory Commission (NRC) has prepared its own cost estimates of nuclear fuel for use in the economic evaluation of nuclear programs. According to NRC the future costs of conversion are expected to remain constant for the next twenty-five years. So far there is a consensus that the future costs of conversion to UF_6 will remain constant. This study assumes that it is reasonable to expect constant production costs in the future.

Fuel Fabrication Costs

Fuel fabrication is the last step in the preparation of the nuclear fuel for delivery to nuclear power plants. Fuel fabrication involves the chemical and mechanical operations needed to prepare the fuel rods and the final assembly for loading them in the power plants. The enriched uranium hexafluoride, UF_6, which is in gaseous form, is converted into uranium dioxide, UO_2, in powder form through a series of operations.[7] The UO_2 is then reduced and compressed into pellets by a series of mechanical operations.

Currently there are thirty fuel fabrication plants in operation in the world, excluding the communist countries. The United States has more than half the world's operating capacity of the fabrication industry.[8] Fuel fabrication technology is highly developed, and the production method is labor intensive. Experience has shown that the cost per unit of output has been declining. A major proportion of the fabrication costs is incurred in connection with the quality assurance requirements of the fuel preparation. The quality control issues are associated with the problems of fuel element failures, early commercial reactor operations, and fuel integrity during the irradiation lifetime. The fabrication industry has been able to provide efficient services to the electric utilities in assuring strict quality control standards. The rapid and unexpected changes in the demand for fuel fabrication services will cancel any economies expected from the operating experience of this industry.

Two types of contracts are used in procuring the services of fuel fabrication: fixed-price contracts and base price contracts. The latter refers to the price prevailing at the time of delivery with some provision for escalation. As an incentive for long-term contracting, fuel manufacturers provide discounts for large reloads of nuclear fuel. A typical base price schedule for UO_2 fuel fabrication for a lightwater reactor for different number of reloads is shown in table 17-1.

The price of UO_2 fuel fabrication declines from $100 per kilogram base price to a low of $67 per kilogram as the number of reloads increases to twelve. A long-term contract for a large number of reloads by electric utilities will promote market stability in the nuclear fuel industry.

As has been the case with UF_6 conversion, fuel fabrication services are not expected to undergo any major changes in their operations that will affect the future costs of fuel production. In 1975 the average fabrication price was

Table 17-1
Prices for UO_2 Fuel Fabrication for Different Number of Reloads
(in 1975 dollars)

Number of Reloads	Base Price ($/kg)
Initial case	$120
Reloads 1	100
2	96
3	93
4	88
5	83
6	80
7	75
8	72
9	69
10	68
11	67
12	67

Source: B. Prince et al., *A Survey of Nuclear Fuel Cycle Economics:* 1970–1985. Oak Ridge National Laboratory, ORNL/TM–5703, March 1977, p. 52.

quoted at $100/kg. The Oak Ridge National Laboratory (ORNL) study forecasts that the fabrication prices will increase to $128 in 1980 and to $163 in 1985. These forecasts assume a 5 percent increase in the fabrication costs each year. The ORNL cost estimates are in current dollars, and the real costs are therefore expected to remain constant given a rate of inflation of 5 percent per year. Similarly the EBASCO study assumes that the fuel fabrication costs will increase at the rate of 4 percent per year. These costs are expected to be $146 in 1986 and $234 in 1998. In both these studies the costs of fabrication, in constant dollars, are expected to remain the same for the next twenty-five years. The Nuclear Regulatory Commission, however, believes that the future fabrication costs per kilogram will decline as experience is gained in this sector of the nuclear fuel cycle.

The cost reductions in fuel fabrication arising from the learning process will be minimal since the technology is already at an advanced stage of development. Any economic gains that may accrue from operating experience may be offset from the fluctuations in the employment of skilled labor in this sector. The present study considers that the fuel fabrication costs, which are estimated to be $93 per kilogram of uranium in 1980, in constant dollars, will remain the same for the next twenty-five years.

Nuclear Fuel Costs

The main focus of this study has been to examine the economic aspects of the nuclear fuel cycle. The costs selected for analysis were the front-end costs of the fuel cycle. The back-end costs of the fuel cycle are the costs of waste management, transportation, and plant decommissioning. The costs of waste management are not known with any certainty and are affected by the policies concerning the recycling and reprocessing of spent fuel. To resolve the uncertainty in the back end of the fuel cycle two methods have been proposed for the calculation of the total nuclear fuel costs.[9] One method requires that a zero value be assigned to the net salvage value of the spent fuel. In this case the option of spent fuel reprocessing is kept open as an economic possibility in the fuel cycle. A decision to recover uranium and plutonium is made when the value of the product recovered exceeds the costs of recovery, waste handling, transportation, and storage. The second method requires that a negative value be assigned to the net slavage value of the nuclear waste. Under this method the recycling and reprocessing option is completely closed in the fuel cycle. The present study assumes that, at least in the near future, reprocessing will not be permitted.

The calculation of the utility nuclear fuel costs require that the front-end costs, back-end costs, and financing costs be known. The financing costs are generally referred to as the indirect costs incurred by the electric utilities in the procurement of nuclear fuel. These costs then become input data to fuel cost computer programs. There are several well-known nuclear fuel cost programs which use different approaches in the estimation of levelized nuclear fuel costs.[10]

Estimates of the fuel costs in mills per kilowatt-hour of electricity generated for the next twenty-five years are unimportant for comparative economic analysis of alternative fuel choices. The future trends in the components of the fuel costs and their relative contribution in the accounting of fuel costs is important in the evaluation of fuel economics. The forecasts of uranium prices and of the services performed in the conversion of nuclear fuel are summarized in table 17-2.

Few studies have attempted to estimate the nuclear fuel costs for the next ten to twenty-five years.[11] A comprehensive analysis of the fuel cost study is currently being carried out by the Nuclear Regulatory Commission. The NRC forecasts of fuel prices are not based on any comprehensive economic studies of fuel cycle operations. The NRC forecasts of uranium prices for the period 1980–2000 are rather unconvincing. The uranium prices are projected to reach $42 per pound of U_3O_8 (in 1977 dollars) in 1980. These prices are expected to remain constant in 1985 and then show a modest increase of $2.70 per pound of U_3O_8 in 1990. The next five years then show a further increase of $2.50 per pound of U_3O_8 in 1995. Between 1995 and 2000 the prices are expected to increase rapidly and reach a high of $59 per pound of U_3O_8. Such a postulated trend in uranium prices during the period 1980–2000 can hardly be justified by any economic reasoning. According to NRC the separative work unit costs are expected to decline after 1990 to a level of costs that will be equivalent to those of 1980. Such a decline in the enrichment costs may not be possible when

Table 17-2
Forecasts of Uranium Prices, Enrichment Costs, UF_6 Conversion Costs, and Fuel Fabrication Costs, 1980–2000
(in 1975 dollars)

	Unit	1980	1985	1990	1995	2000
Uranium prices						
High case	Dollars per	28	37	47	55	59
Base case	pound of	25	32	36	42	47
Low case	U_3O_8	23	28	33	36	40
Separative work unit	Dollars per SWU	100	100	100	100	100
Conversion to UF_6	Dollars per kilogram of U	4.6	4.6	4.6	4.6	4.6
Fuel fabrication costs	Dollars per kilogram of U	93	93	93	93	93

the accounting of enrichment costs is further revised to conform with the commercial operations of the private sector. The NRC forecasts of fuel prices are compared with the forecasts of the present study in figure 17-1.

A pertinent issue in this analysis is the economic implications of the nuclear fuel costs on the decisions made by the electric utilities in the evaluation of optimum fuel choice. The estimates of nuclear fuel costs for the next twenty to thirty years do not themselves provide a rational basis for the economic assessment of nuclear technology. For a meaningful economic analysis, the costs of nuclear and coal should be examined well into the future from the point of future costs of electricity generation. The relative costs of nuclear and coal

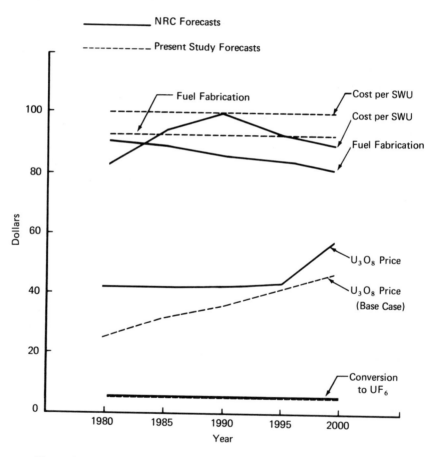

Figure 17-1. Alternate Forecasts of Front-End Fuel Costs, 1980-2000

are the important ones in determining the economic advantage of these fuels in electricity generation. Economic studies pertaining to the long-term contribution of coal in electricity generation have expressed serious doubts concerning the capability of the coal industry to meet its relative share of electricity generation in 1985 and beyond.[12] The uncertainties surrounding the future of coal supplies may cause the differential costs between coal and nuclear to widen in favor of the nuclear option.

Notes

1. The Nuclear Regulatory Commission assumes that the back-end costs of the fuel cycle will remain constant for the next twenty to thirty years (private communications with Theodore Workinger of the Technology Assessment Division of the Nuclear Regulatory Commission).

2. A detailed description of technologies is found in U.S. Atomic Energy Commission, *Environmental Survey of the Uranium Fuel Cycle.* WASH-1248, April 1974, pp. C-1 to C-26. See also *Nuclear Energy,* Central Intelligence Agency. ER77-10468, August 1977.

3. B. Prince et al., *A Survey of Nuclear Fuel Cycle Economics 1970-1985.* Oak Ridge National Laboratory, ORNL/TM-5703, March 1977.

4. AEC, *Environmental Survey.*

5. Prince et al., *A Survey,* pp. 46-52.

6. A.J. Rossi and F.A. Ritchings, "Dramatic Changes in Nuclear and Fossil Costs," paper presented at 47th Annual Executive Conference, Hilton Head Island, South Carolina, EBASCO Services, October 1976.

7. AEC, *Environmental Survey.*

8. Ibid.

9. Prince et al., *A Survey*

10. R. Salmon, *User's Manual for REFCO, A Discounted Cash Flow Code for Calculating Nuclear Fuel Cycle Costs,* ORNL/TM-3709, April 1972; *Nuclear Fuel Economics,* Nuclear Fuel Division, Westinghouse Electric Corporation, 1974.

11. Prince et al., *A Survey;* Rossi and Ritchings, "Dramatic Changes"; also R.L. Gordon, *U.S. Coal and Electric Power Industry,* Johns Hopkins Press, Baltimore, Md., 1975.

12. *U.S. Coal Development—Promises, Uncertainties,* U.S. General Accounting Office, September 22, 1977. For an economic comparison of nuclear and coal plants, see A.D. Rossin and T.A. Rieck, "Economics of Nuclear Power," *Science,* August 18, 1978, pp. 582-589.

18 Nuclear Option in Energy Policy

A number of studies have proposed different options for nuclear development in the Carter administration's national energy plan. Many of these proposals are based on certain assumptions regarding the availability of technology and resource, economics, and environmental considerations. This study briefly reviews the role of nuclear in the energy plan in relation to the economic aspects of the nuclear fuel industry.

The availability of the uranium resource has been a critical factor in the economic evaluation of alternative nuclear technologies in the nation's energy planning. Another factor that has received equally serious attention is the cost of nuclear fuel for the plants in operation in the year 2000. Any possible changes in the structure and organization of the production of uranium ore and nuclear fuel that affect the allocative efficiency of resources and the prices of fuel have also become matters of national interest. The results of this study are evaluated in relation to some of these issues.

Nuclear Fuel Supplies

A survey of the conventional and nonconventional uranium deposits indicates that the United States possesses adequate uranium resources to provide the fuel needs of the projected nuclear capacity to the year 2000. The cumulative uranium requirements, assuming no recycling and reprocessing, can be met from the domestic uranium reserves and resources. Future discoveries of low-grade sandstone deposits are possible. In addition to the known sandstone deposits, large quantities of uranium are available as a by-product of the wet phosphoric acid processes and copper leach operations. Future developments in world uranium production and trade will provide more choices in meeting the future fuel needs of the U.S. nuclear industry.

The mere abundance of uranium resource cannot be used as a basis for advocating the continuation of lightwater reactor fission programs for the next several hundred years. Several factors, besides resource adequacy, will impede the continuation of fission programs as long-term nuclear option in the national energy plans. The major problems that will constrain the feasibility of the lightwater reactors are the issues dealing with the disposal of ore tailings, nuclear waste management, and the dismantling and decommissioning of older nuclear plants. These problems cannot be regarded as insurmountable for nuclear capacity, which can be expected to be only as high as 400 MW to 600 MW. The amount of nuclear waste generated by the nuclear plants in the year 2000 is expected to be as little as 1 percent of the total waste generated from the nuclear weapons programs.[1]

Another aspect of the supply analysis is the reliability of the fuel supplies to the electric utilities. The nuclear fuel cycle is different from the coal cycle since a great deal of processing is required before uranium is delivered as fuel to the power plants. The long lead times required at each stage of the fuel processing generally make the utilities procure long-term nuclear fuel supplies for the power plants in operation and under construction. Approximately two years are required between the time uranium is procured from the uranium mines and the final delivery of fuel batches to reactors. Electric utilities are provided with a minimum of two year's nuclear fuel supplies for the operation of the power plants. Therefore the disruptions in the supply of uranium production at mines and mills are not likely to have major impacts on the scheduling and operation of the nuclear power plants. Cutbacks in uranium production because of labor strikes and for similar reasons cannot have severe and sudden effects on the national economy, as has been the case with the oil and coal. These special characteristics of nuclear make it a much more attractive option for enhancing the nation's reliability of fuel supplies to electric power stations.

Role of Government

Unlike many natural resource industries, the uranium mining and milling industry has been developed, protected, and promoted by the federal government. The production of nuclear fuel is entirely in the hands of the private sector, with the exception of the uranium enrichment operations. Since the nuclear fuel cycle operations are so closely related to matters of national and international security, the federal government will continue to monitor commercial transactions in the fuel cycle. A much more important role for government is insuring the stability of nuclear operations and restoring the workability of the competitive markets in the nuclear industry. The stability of market conditions can be envisioned if a firm commitment to nuclear development is made, through legislation of regulatory measures for expediency and acceptability of nuclear as a part of the total energy system. The process of assuring the competitiveness of the market system in the nuclear fuel industry is complicated.

There is a widely held belief that the market operations in the uranium mining and milling industry may have been ineffective because of possible concentration of market power in the hands of a few producers. The economic basis for such a conclusion requires a detailed analysis of the industry structure. Possible producers' collusion can be inferred from the future trend in the prices of uranium. If the actual uranium prices differ by a substantial margin from the forecasts of uranium prices provided in this study, then some doubts can be raised concerning the effectiveness of the market systems in the uranium-mining industry. The government should also encourage economic studies of the uranium industry focusing on the future patterns of production and prices.

As a measure of economic stability in the nuclear fuel industry, the government should encourage and facilitate the purchases of uranium reserves by the electric utilities. This policy will help stabilize the flow of uranium concentrate in the nuclear fuel cycle. In the same manner the government can help assure the stability of the domestic uranium markets by encouraging foreign imports of uranium. The possibility of an international uranium cartel does not constitute a real threat to the energy independence of the U.S. economy. The adequacy of the resource base and the advanced technological status of the U.S. nuclear fuel industry can always thwart any such adverse action by an outside uranium cartel.

The enrichment operations currently owned and operated by the federal government should continue to serve the needs of the U.S. and foreign electric utilities. The decline in the demand for nuclear power has considerably slowed the urgent need for additional plants in the very near future. The federal government which once proposed to assure the entry of private industry should discourage private participation in the operations of enrichment plants. In the long run the social costs of providing safeguards for any misuse of enrichment technology in private hands will far exceed the expected benefits to the U.S. economy. The government should carefully evaluate the question of enrichment technology transfer to the private sector even without any assurances or provisions for risk in fuel production. The survey of enrichment operations indicates that the federal government can improve the economic performance of the government-owned enrichment plants by instituting procedures that conform to management practices used in the private sector.

The management and operations of the other sectors of the fuel economy, UF_6 conversion and fuel fabrication, show no need for government involvement. Finally the role of the government should be to monitor operations and manage nuclear fuel to assure the workability of the market systems and safeguard the proper use of nuclear material as a fuel for power plants.

Nuclear Power and Energy Policy

The national energy plan has evolved through a series of legislative debates that reflect the preferences of several interest groups.[2] The plan emphasizes the need for less reliance on foreign imports of oil and the maximum productive utilization of domestic coal, oil, and natural gas resources. The contributions of the lightwater reactor industry are significant in the achievement of certain goals of this policy. The nuclear option provides a groundwork for the country to make a transition from an oil-dependent nation to one whose energy needs are met from inexhaustible energy sources. Solar and fusion technologies are undoubtedly regarded as the most promising future energy sources in the U.S. economy. A transition to solar and fusion is not possible for at least the next twenty to thirty years. During this interim period the U.S. economy remains heavily dependent on foreign oil, which has become a problem of serious economic concern in the national energy plan. The depletion of world oil resources and the expected rapid increases in oil prices caused by OPEC action and by future oil scarcity are likely to compound the economic crisis and seriously strain the functioning of the U.S. economy. The present fission industry is a short-term provision enabling the U.S. economy to make proper adjustments in the transition to nonfossil energy future. A possible slack in the contributions of coal can be taken up by the lightwater reactor industry during the next twenty years.

The preservation of the present generation of lightwater reactors to the year 2000 provides sufficient time for the country to consider the development of long-term nuclear strategies in the growth of the U.S. economy. Prudent and rational planning requires that all nuclear options be examined from economic, environmental, and national security considerations. The major competing long-term nuclear options that could become economically feasible (some are already in operation and commercially feasible) beyond the year 2000 are lightwater reactor systems, proliferation-resistant systems, plutonium breeders, and fusion. An evaluation of the relative merits of each option in an economic framework assessing the social benefits and costs is beyond the scope of this work. However, such a measure will be necessary in determining the relative priorities that must be assigned for funding the reaearch-and-development aspects of these technologies. This review is intended to rank these technologies in order of real cost to the society primarily from the point of uranium resource dependency and economics of fuel. The world economic future, a hundred years from now, would be much different from today's in terms of growth, interdependencies, resource control, and international trade. But some major decisions that affect the selection and promotion of alternative nuclear technologies are necessary at the present time. These remarks should not be considered definitive; instead they should be taken merely as portrayals of the best futures on the basis of existing scenarios of the national economy

One of the long-term nuclear options is a continuation of the present generation of reactors, which consist mostly of pressurized water reactors and boiling water reactors using the once-through fuel cycle.[3] However, these reactors are regarded as inefficient from the standpoint of uranium consumption. If these reactors continue to be installed beyond 2000, then the currently identified uranium reserves and resources from conventional sources can fuel not more than six hundred to seven hundred thousand megawatts of nuclear capacity. The extrapolation of the lightwater reactor capacity beyond 2000 poses several difficult questions. Therefore the continuation of the lightwater reactors using the once-through fuel cycle should be regarded as the least socially desirable nuclear option.

Another long-term nuclear option suggests a shift from the current light-water reactors to the already established, uranium efficient, heavy water reactors commonly known as CANDU. The heavy water reactors operating on an isotopically denatured uranium-thorium fuel cycle are considered efficient in uranium use. These proliferation-resistant nuclear systems are considered three to five times more efficient than their counterpart lightwater reactors on once-through fuel cycles.[4] An adoption of these programs would extend the present supplies of uranium resources and make the nuclear systems proliferation resistant, deterring the spread of nuclear weapons and terrorism. However, these programs will not eliminate resource dependency, and the unanswered question, What next? will remain a major issue with an alarming need and urgency. Therefore these programs should be promoted as hedges against the possible failure of fusion technology, which is an ultimate source of power for the survival of mankind. In the event that nuclear fusion and nuclear breeders do not become a reality in the U.S. energy economy, the proliferation resistant programs should be accorded highest priority.

Nuclear breeders, which would free the energy economy from the uranium resource constraints, have been plagued with problems of economics, safety, environment, and proliferation of nuclear weapons.[5] There are different types of breeders and the ones under some degree of development are the LMFBR (liquid metal fast breeder), GCFR (gas-cooled fast breeder), MSBR (molten-salt breeder), and LWBR (lightwater breeder). The LMFBR has been pursued aggressively to bring it into operation by a specific date. The nuclear breeder has been considered an economic necessity becuase fission reactors cannot support the ever-increasing electric energy demand from a limited uranium resource base. The recent declines in U.S. electric energy demand and the discovery of large uranium resources in recent years make the commercial entry of breeders in the near future an economic luxury. However, the breeder option should not be closed permanently. If nuclear fusion fails, breeders should be encouraged for commercial entry at a pace commensurate with the technical and institutional capabilities of the U.S. economy while the resolution of several major issues in this field is sought.

There are different concepts of fusion reactor technology, with different fuel cycles, different modes of operation and confinement, and different types of energy conversion cycles. First-generation reactors will use the deuterium-tritium fuel cycle and produce tritium in the reactor blanket by the interaction of neutrons and lithium. Fusion power is considered the most socially desirable option because there are fewer radioactive products than with fission power. Fusion relieves the dependency on fuel supply since tritium occurs in abundant supply in all water, and there is sufficient deuterium for a very large fusion power industry.[6] Fusion is therefore a highly preferred long-term nuclear alternative.

The continuation of fission reactors for the next thirty years will provide a great deal of flexibility in the selection of alternative nuclear technologies. The significance of lightwater reactors in the U.S. energy economy for the next thirty years should not be dismissed. The nation should preserve this nuclear fission alternative as it preserves the economic integrity of the energy economy.

Notes

1. The degree of radiation hazard from the wastes produced in commercial sector is said to be roughly equal to the hazard from the wastes resulting from military operations. The problem of waste management can be viewed as a sociopolitical one. For alternative approaches to waste management, see T.R. La Porte, "Nuclear Waste: Increasing Scale and Sociopolitical Impacts," *Science*, July 7, 1978, pp. 22-28.

2. *The National Energy Plan*, Executive Office of the President, Energy Policy and Planning, 1977.

3. For a list of alternative fuel cycles, see Energy Research and Development Administration, *Nonproliferation Alternative Systems Assessment Program*, Preliminary Program Plan, May 1977.

4. H.A. Feiverson et al., *An Evolutionary Strategy for Nuclear Power: Alternatives to Breeders*, Program on Nuclear Policy Alternatives, Center for Environmental Studies, Princeton University, Princeton, N.J., June 1978.

5. J.E. Gray et al., *International Cooperation on Breeder Reactors*, Rockefeller Foundation, May 1978.

6. S.B. Ahmed, "Role of Nuclear Power: 1985-2040," *Public Utilities Fortnightly*, May 22, 1975; S.E. Beall et al., *An Assessment of the Environmental Impacts of Alternative Sources of Energy*, 5024, Oak Ridge National Laboratory, Oak Ridge, Tennessee, August 1975.

Bibliography

Ahmed, S.B. "Role of Nuclear Power: 1985–2040." *Public Utilities Fortnightly,* May 22, 1975.

Arnold, W.H. "On the Subject of Nuclear Reactor Operating Experience." Testimony before the Assembly Committee on Resources, Land Use, and Energy. Sacramento, California, October 1975.

Atomic Industrial Forum, Inc. *Report on the Seminar on Uranium.* Program Report, March 1973.

Beall, S.E. Spiewak, I., Arnold, H.G., McLain, H.W., Bettis, E.S., Scott, D., Ahmed, S.B. *An Assessment of the Environmental Impacts of Alternate Sources of Energy,* 5024, Oak Ridge National Laboratory, August 1975.

Bender, M., and Ahmed, S.B. *Index of the Composite Environment (ICE): A Basis for Evaluating Environmental Effects of Electric Power Generating Plants in Response to NEPA.* Oak Ridge National Laboratory, TM–4492, February 1974.

Blumkin, S. *Survey of Foreign Enrichment Capacity Contracting and Technology: January 1976–December 1976.* Oak Ridge Gaseous Diffusion Plant, Oak Ridge, Tennessee, April 1977.

Brush, Harvey F. "Power Plant Economics." Testimony before the Connecticut Public Utilities Control Authority, January 21, 1976.

Breyer, S.G., and MacAvoy, P.W. *Energy Regulation by the Federal Power Commission.* Brookings Institution, Washington, D.C., 1974.

Bureau of Mines. *Mineral Facts and Problems.* Bulletin 650, U.S. Department of the Interior, Washington, D.C., 1970.

Bureau of Mines. *Supply and Demand for Energy in the United States by States and Regions, 1960 and 1965,* U.S. Department of the Interior, Washington, D.C., 1975.

Bupp, Irving C. "The Economics of Nuclear Power," *Technol. Rev.* 77 (1975):

Chern, W.S. *Electricity Demand by Manufacturing Industries in the United States,* ORNL/NSF/EP-87.

Council on Wage and Price Stability, Staff Report. *A Study of Coal Prices,* Executive Office of the President, March 1976.

Davis, W.K. "Economics of Nuclear Power." Paper presented at International Symposium on Nuclear Power Technology and Economics, January 13, 1975.

Deonigi, D.E., and Engel, R.L. "The Economics of Fusion-Fission Systems." Mimeographed. Battelle Pacific Northwest Laboratories, Richland, Washington.

Deonigi, D.E., and Engel, R.L. "Performance Targets for Fusion-Fission (Hybrid) Reactors." Mimeographed. Battelle Pacific Northwest Laboratories, Richland, Washington, January 1977.

EBASCO Services, Inc. *Fossil and Nuclear 1000-NW Central Station Power Plants Investment Estimates.* 1975.

Edison Electric Institute. *Nuclear Fuels Supply.* New York, March 1976.

Energy Research and Development Administration. *Expansion of U.S. Enrichment Capacity.* Draft Environmental Statement, ERDA-1543, June 1975.

Energy Research and Development Administration. *ORCOST II: A Computer Code for Estimating the Cost of Power from Steam Electric Power Plants.* ERDA-76/38, October 1975.

Energy Research and Development Administration. *Report of the Liquid Metal Fast Breeder Reactor Program—Review Group.* ERDA-1, January 1975.

Energy Research and Development Administration. *Statistical Data of the Uranium Industry.* GJO-100(75)/(76), 1975, 1976, Grand Junction Office, Grand Junction, Colorado, January 1, 1976.

Energy Research and Development Administration. *Survey of United States Uranium Marketing Activity.* 1973, 1975, 1976.

Energy Research and Development Administration, *U.S. Nuclear Power Export Activities.* Final Environmental Statement, ERDA-1542.

Energy Research and Development Administration. *Uranium Enrichment Conference.* CONF-751134, Oak Ridge, Tennessee, November 1975.

Energy Research and Development Administration. *Uranium Industry Seminar.* GJO-108(75), Grand Junction Office, October 1975.

Erickson, Edward, et al. "Oil Supply and Tax Incentives." *Brookings Papers on Economic Activity,* Brookings Institution, Washington, D.C., 1974.

Fisher, F.M., Cootner, P.H., and Bailey, M.N. "An Econometric Model of the World Copper Industry." *Bell J. Econ.,* 3 (1972):568–609.

Foster Associates, Inc. *Energy Prices 1960-1973.* A Report to the Energy Policy Project of the Ford Foundation. Ballinger Publishing Company, Cambridge, Mass., 1974.

Gordon, Richard L. *U.S. Coal and the Electric Power Industry.* Johns Hopkins University Press, Baltimore, Md., 1975.

Jaskow, P.L. and Baughman, M.L. "The Future of the U.S. Nuclear Energy Industry." *Bell J. Econ.* 7 (1976).

Johnson, J. *Econometric Methods.* McGraw-Hill, New York, 1963.

Jorgenson, D.W. *Econometric Studies of U.S. Energy Policy.* North-Holland, Amsterdam, 1976.

Kelejian, Harry H. "Two-Stage Least Squares and Econometric Systems Linear in Parameters But Nonlinear in the Endogenous Variables." *J. Am. Stat. Assoc.* 66 (1971):373–374.

Kennedy, M. "An Economic Model of the World Oil Market." *Bell J. Econ.* 5 (1974):540–577.

Keyfitz, N. *Introduction to the Population of Mathematics.* Addison-Wesley, Reading, Massachusetts, 1968.

Kiser, E.B. "Review of U.S. Gas Centrifuge Program." Paper presented at Fuel Cycle Conference, Atomic Industrial Forum, 1977.

Labys, W.C. *Dynamic Commodity Models: Specifications, Estimations, and Simulation.* Lexington Books, D.C. Heath and Co., Lexington, Mass. 1973.

Labys, W.C. *Quantitative Models of Commodity Markets.* Ballinger Publishing Company, Cambridge, Mass., 1975.

MacAvoy, Paul R. *Economic Strategy for Developing Nuclear Breeder Reactors.* MIT Press, Cambridge, Mass., 1969.

May, R.M. *Model Ecosystem.* Princeton University Press, Princeton, N.J., 1973.

National Academy of Sciences. *Mineral Resources and the Environment, Reserves and Resources of Uranium in the United States,* Washington, D.C., 1975.

National Petroleum Council. *U.S. Energy Outlook: Nuclear Energy Availability.* 1973.

OECD Nuclear Energy Agency and the International Atomic Energy Agency. *Uranium: Resources, Production and Demand,* Paris, December 1975, 1977.

Pindyck, R.S., and Rubinfield, D. *Econometric Models and Economic Forecasts.* McGraw-Hill, New York, 1976.

Pindyck, R.S. "The Regulatory Implications of Three Alternative Econometric Supply Models of Natural Gas." *Bell J. Econ.* 5 (1974):633–645.

Price, W.J. "Reprocessing Incentives." *Fuel Cycle Conference 1976,* Atomic Industrial Forum, Phoenix, Arizona, March 1976.

Reichle, L.F.C. "The Economics of Nuclear Power." Mimeograph. New York Society of Security Analysts. vol. 77, August 27, 1975.

Salmon R. *User's Manual for REFCO; A Discounted Cash Flow Code for Calculating Nuclear Fuel Cycle Costs,* ORNL/TM-3709, April 1972.

Searl, M.F. and Platt, J. "Views on Uranium and Thorium Resources." *Ann. Nucl. Energy* 2 (1975):751–762.

Stauffer, T.R., Palmer, R.S., and Lyckoff, H.L. *Breeder Reactor Economics,* Breeder Reactor Corporation, July 1975.

U.S. Atomic Energy Commission. *NUFUEL, Computer Program for Forecasting Nuclear Fuel Requirements and Related Quantities.* WASH-1348, October 1974.

U.S. Atomic Energy Commission. *Nuclear Fuel Resources and Requirements.* WASH-1243, April 1973.

U.S. Atomic Energy Commission. *Power Plant Capital Costs; Current Trends and Sensitivity to Economic Parameters.* WASH-1345, October 1974.

U.S. Atomic Energy Commission. *Environmental Survey of the Uranium Fuel Cycle.* WASH-1248, April 1974.

U.S. Department of Commerce, Bureau of the Census, *Statistical Abstract of the United States, 1975.*

U.S. Department of the Interior. *United States Energy Fact Sheet.* February 1973.

Vanstrum, P.R., and Levin, S.A. "New Processes for Uranium Isotope Separation." IAEA–CN–36/12(11.3), December 1976.

Vogley, W.A. *Mineral Materials Modeling.* John Hopkins University Press, Baltimore, Md., 1975.

Wallace, W.H., Nayler, T.H., and Sasser, W.E. "An Econometric Model of the Textile Industry in the United States." *Rev. Econ. Stat.* 50 (1968):13–22.

Wallis, K.F. *Introductory Econometrics.* Aldine Publishing, Chicago, 1972.

Westley, G.W. *SAMPLE: A Two Stage Least Squares Program with Data Transportation Capabilities.* ORNL/NSF/EP–28, Oak Ridge National Laboratory, December 1972.

Wilson, C.L. *Energy: Global Prospects, 1985–2000.* Report of the Workshop on Alternative Energy Strategies, McGraw-Hill, New York, 1977.

Index

About the Author

S. Basheer Ahmed is professor of economics at Western Kentucky University. He received the B.A. from Madras University, India, the M.A. from Osmania University, India, and the M.S. and Ph.D. from Texas A & M University. He completed this book while he was a Visiting Fellow at the Center of International Studies, Princeton University. Dr. Ahmed has served as a consultant to various federal government and research organizations, and is vice-president of the Systems, Man, and Cybernetics Society of the Institute of Electrical and Electronics Engineers. He is also a member of the American Nuclear Society and a Fellow of the American Association for the Advancement of Science. Dr. Ahmed has published numerous articles in professional journals in the areas of economics, energy, and mathematical programming.

Center of International Studies: List of Publications

Gabriel A. Almond, *The Appeals of Communism* (Princeton University Press 1954)

William W. Kaufmann, ed., *Military Policy and National Security* (Princeton University Press 1956)

Klaus Knorr, *The War Potential of Nations* (Princeton University Press 1956)

Lucian W. Pye, *Guerrilla Communism in Malaya* (Princeton University Press 1956)

Charles De Visscher, *Theory and Reality in Public International Law*, trans. P.E. Corbett (Princeton University Press 1957; rev. ed. 1968)

Bernard C. Cohen, *The Political Process and Foreign Policy: The Making of the Japanese Peace Settlement* (Princeton University Press 1957)

Myron Weiner, *Party Politics in India: The Development of a Multi-Party System* (Princeton University Press 1957)

Percy E. Corbett, *Law in Diplomacy* (Princeton University Press 1959)

Rolf Sannwald and Jacques Stohler, *Economic Integration: Theoretical Assumptions and Consequences of European Unification*, trans. Herman Karreman (Princeton University Press 1959)

Klaus Knorr, ed., *NATO and American Security* (Princeton University Press 1959)

Gabriel A. Almond and James S. Coleman, ed., *The Politics of the Developing Areas* (Princeton University Press 1960)

Herman Kahn, *On Thermonuclear War* (Princeton University Press 1960)

Sidney Verba, *Small Groups and Political Behavior: A Study of Leadership* (Princeton University Press 1961)

Robert J.C. Butow, *Tojo and the Coming of the War* (Princeton University Press 1961)

Glenn H. Snyder, *Deterrence and Defense: Toward a Theory of National Security* (Princeton University Press, 1961)

Klaus Knorr and Sidney Verba, ed., *The International System: Theoretical Essays* (Princeton University Press 1961)

Peter Paret and John W. Shy, *Guerrillas in the 1960's* (Praeger 1962)

George Modelski, *A Theory of Foreign Policy* Praeger, 1962)

Klaus Knorr and Thornton Read, eds., *Limited Strategic War* (Praeger 1963)

Frederick S. Dunn, *Peace-Making and the Settlement with Japan* (Princeton University Press 1963)

Arthur L. Burns and Nina Heathcote, *Peace-Keeping by United Nations Forces* (Praeger 1963)

Richard A. Falk, *Law, Morality, and War in the Contemporary World* (Praeger, 1963)

James N. Rosenau, *National Leadership and Foreign Policy: A Case Study in the Mobilization of Public Support* (Princeton University Press 1963)

Gabriel A. Almond and Sidney Verba, *The Civic Culture: Political Attitudes and Democracy in Five Nations* (Princeton University Press 1963)

Bernard C. Cohen, *The Press and Foreign Policy* (Princeton University Press 1963)

Richard L. Sklar, *Nigerian Political Parties: Power in an Emergent African Nation* (Princeton University Press 1963)

Peter Paret, *French Revolutionary Warfare from Indochina to Algeria: The Analysis of a Political and Military Doctrine* (Praeger 1964)

Harry Eckstein, ed., *Internal War: Problems and Approaches* (Free Press 1964)

Cyril E. Black and Thomas P. Thornton, ed., *Communism and Revolution: The Strategic Uses of Political Violence* (Princeton University Press 1964)

Miriam Camps, *Britain and the European Community 1955-1963* (Princeton University Press 1964)

Thomas P. Thornton, ed., *The Third World in Soviet Perspective: Studies by Soviet Writers on the Developing Areas* (Princeton University Press 1964)

James N. Rosenau, ed., *International Aspects of Civl Strife* (Princeton University Press 1964)

Sidney I. Ploss, *Conflict and Decision-Making in Soviet Russia: A Case Study of Agricultural Policy, 1953-1963* (Princeton University Press 1965)

Richard A. Falk and Richard J. Barnet, ed., *Security in Disarmament* (Princeton University Press 1965)

Karl von Vorys, *Political Development in Pakistan* (Princeton University Press 1965)

Harold and Margaret Sprout, *The Ecological Perspective on Human Affairs, with Special Reference to International Politics* (Princeton University Press 1965)

Klaus Knorr, *On the Uses of Military Power in the Nuclear Age* (Princeton University Press 1966)

Harry Eckstein, *Division and Cohesion in Democracy: A Study of Norway* (Princeton University Press 1966)

Cyril E. Black, *Th Dynamics of Modernization: A Study in Comparative History* (Harper and Row 1966)

Peter Kunstadter, ed., *Southeast Asian Tribes, Minorities, and Nations* (Princeton University Press 1967)

E. Victor Wolfenstein, *The Revolutionary Personality: Lenin, Trotsky, Gandhi* (Princeton University Press 1967)

Leon Gordenker, *The UN Secretary-General and the Maintenance of Peace* (Columbia University Press 1967)

Oran R. Young, *The Intermediaries: Third Parties in International Crises* (Princeton University Press 1967)

James N. Rosenau, ed., *Domestic Sources of Foreign Policy* (Free Press 1967)

Richard F. Hamilton, *Affluence and the French Worker in the Fourth Republic* (Princeton University Press 1967)

Linda B. Miller, *World Order and Local Disorder: The United Nations and Internal Conflicts* (Princeton University Press 1967)

Henry Bienen, *Tanzania: Party Transformation and Economic Development* (Princeton University Press 1967)

Wolfram F. Hanrieder, *West German Foreign Policy, 1949–1963: International Pressures and Domestic Response* (Stanford University Press 1967)

Richard H. Ullman, *Britain and the Russian Civil War: November 1918–February 1920* (Princeton University Press 1968)

Robert Gilpin, *France in the Age of the Scientific State* (Princeton University Press 1968)

William B. Bader, *The United States and the Spread of Nuclear Weapons* (Pegasus 1968)

Richard A. Falk, *Legal Order in a Violent World* (Princeton University Press 1968)

Cyril E. Black, Richard A. Falk, Klaus Knorr, and Oran R. Young, *Neutralization and World Politics* (Princeton University Press 1968)

Oran R. Young, *The Politics of Force: Bargaining during International Crises* (Princeton University Press 1969)

Klaus Knorr and James N. Rosenau, eds., *Contending Approaches to International Politics* (Princeton University Press 1969)

James N. Rosenau, ed., *Linkage Politics: Essays on the Convergence of National and International Systems* (Free Press 1969)

John T. McAlister, Jr., *Viet Nam: The Origins of Revolution* (Knopf 1969)

Jean Edward Smith, *Germany Beyond the Wall: People, Politics, and Prosperity* (Little, Brown 1969)

James Barros, *Betrayal from Within: Joseph Avenol, Secretary-General of the League of Nations, 1933–1940* (Yale University Press 1969)

Charles Hermann, *Crisis in Foreign Policy: A Simulation Analysis* (Bobbs-Merrill 1960)

Robert C. Tucker, *The Marxian Revolutionary Idea: Essays on Marxist Thought and Its Impact on Radical Movements* (W.W. Norton 1969)

Harvey Waterman, *Political Change in Contemporary France: The Politics of an Industrial Democracy* (Charles E. Merrill 1969)

Cyril E. Black and Richard A. Falk, eds., *The Future of the International Legal Order,* Vol. 1: *Trends and Patterns* (Princeton University Press 1969)

Ted Robert Gurr, *Why Men Rebel* (Princeton University Press 1969)

C. Sylvester Whitaker, *The Politics of Tradition: Continuity and Change in Northern Nigeria 1946–1966* (Princeton University Press 1970)

Richard A. Falk, *The Status of Law in International Society* (Princeton University Press 1970)

Klaus Knorr, *Military Power and Potential* (D.C. Heath 1970)

Cyril E. Black and Richard A. Falk, eds., *The Futre of the International Legal Order*. Vol. 2: *Wealth and Resources* (Princeton University Press 1970)

Leon Gordenker, ed., *The United Nations in International Politics* (Princeton University Press 1971)

Cyril E. Black and Richard A. Falk, eds., *The Future of the International Legal Order*. Vol. 3: *Conflict Management* (Princeton University Press 1971)

Francine R. Frankel, *India's Green Revolution: Political Costs of Economic Growth* (Princeton University Press 1971)

Harold and Margaret Sprout, *Toward a Politics of the Planet Earth* (Van Nostrand Reinhold 1971)

Cyril E. Black and Richard A. Falk, eds., *The Future of the International Legal Order*. Vol 4: *The Structure of the International Environment* (Princeton University Press 1972)

Gerald Garvey, *Energy, Ecology, Economy* (W.W. Norton 1972)

Richard Ullman, *The Anglo-Soviet Accord* (Princeton University Press 1973)

Klaus Knorr, *Power and Wealth: The Political Economy of International Power* (Basic Books 1973)

Anton Bebler, *Military Rule in Africa: Dahomey, Ghana, Sierra Leone, and Mali* (Praeger 1973)

Robert C. Tucker, *Stalin as Revolutionary 1879–1929: A Study in History and Personality* (W.W. Norton 1973)

Edward L. Morse, *Foreign Policy and Interdependence in Gaullist France* (Princeton University Press 1973)

Henry Bienen, *Kenya: The Politics of Participation and Control* (Princeton University Press 1974)

Gregory J. Massell, *The Surrogate Proletariat: Moslem Women and Revolutionary Strategies in Soviet Central Asia, 1919–1929* (Princeton University Press 1974)

James Rosenau, *Citizenship between Elections: An Inquiry into the Mobilizable American* (Free Press 1974)

Ervin Laszio, *A Strategy For the Future: The Systems Approach to World Order* (Braziller 1974)

John R. Vincent, *Nonintervention and International Order* (Princeton University Press 1974)

Jan H. Kalicki, *The Pattern of Sino-American Crises: Political-Military Interactions in the 1950s* (Cambridge University Press 1975)

Klaus Knorr, *The Power of Nations: The Political Economy of International Relations* (Basic Books 1975)

James P. Sewell, *UNESCO and World Politics: Engaging in International Relations* (Princeton University Press 1975)

Richard A. Falk, *A Gobal Approach to National Policy* (Harvard University Press 1975)

Harry Eckstein and Ted Robert Gurr, *Patterns of Authority: A Structural Basis for Political Inquiry* (John Wiley and Sons 1975)

Cyril E. Black, Marius B. Jansen, Herbert S. Levine, Marion J. Levy, Jr., Henry Rosovsky, Gilbert Rozman, Henry D. Smith, II, and S. Frederick Starr, *The Modernization of Japan and Russia* (Free Press 1975)

Leon Gordenker, *International Aid and National Decisions: Development Programs in Malawi, Tanzania, and Zambia* (Princeton University Press 1976)

Carl Von Clausewitz, *On War,* ed. and trans. Michael Howard and Peter Paret (Princeton University Press 1976)

Gerald Garvey and Lou Ann Garvey, eds., *International Resource Flows* (Lexington Books, D.C. Heath 1977)

Gerald Garvey, *Nuclear Power and Social Planning* (Lexington Books, D.C. Heath 1977)